easy weekend
CROCHET HATS

easy weekend
CROCHET
HATS

A SKI-STYLE COLLECTION
FOR THE ENTIRE FAMILY

Jennifer J. Cirka

Fons&Porter

CINCINNATI, OHIO

contents

introduction

When I moved to Colorado from Western Pennsylvania back in December of 1996, I simply wasn't prepared for the amount of time I would spend outdoors. In Colorado, as long as the sun is shining (which it is 70 percent of the time in Western Colorado), people are outdoors. No longer could I hibernate in my house from October to May. Suddenly I found myself mountain biking, hiking, rafting and camping in the summer; skiing, snowboarding, snowshoeing and sledding in the winter. As an avid crocheter, I jumped at the chance to create hats for all of these activities.

The hats in this book are designed to keep you and your family warm and stylish, whether you need to cover your helmet hair after an amazing mountain bike adventure, keep the sun off your head while hiking, look hip while shredding down the snowy mountains or simply shop around a fabulous ski town while sipping hot cocoa. Wherever you enjoy the outdoors, enjoy it in one of these hats!

getting started

Before you jump into these projects, there are a few things you should know: how to pick the right crochet hook, which yarns are best suited for hats, what size is right for you, how to make a pom-pom, etc. Never fear—I've covered all that and more in the following pages.

tools

Imagine that you are a mechanic: you're not going to take off a lug nut with a hammer, are you? Or, what if that inexpensive ratchet breaks just as you are about to get that pesky socket loose enough to remove. Frustrating, isn't it? Whether you are working on a car or crocheting a beautiful hat, you need to choose your tools wisely. Good tools make the job more pleasurable. You want your tools to be comfortable to work with and a good fit for you and your project. Choose wisely, and of course, using visually pleasing tools doesn't hurt either.

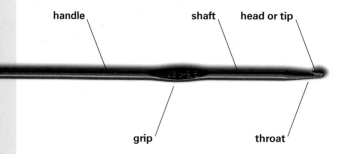

handle   shaft   head or tip

grip   throat

PARTS OF A CROCHET HOOK

✳ TIPS AND TRICKS

When crocheting, try to keep the yarn loop on the shaft of the hook. This will ensure that your stitches are the correct size and keep your stitches uniform.

HOOKS

Crochet hooks come in many different varieties, but they often have the same things in common. The average crochet hook is made up of five to six basic parts: the head or tip, the throat, the shaft, the handle, and some may or may not have a thumb rest or grip.

Most yarn hooks have one of two different head shapes: round or in-line (which is sometimes called flat). A common name brand for round head hooks is Boye and a common name brand for in-line hooks is Susan Bates. Both of these brands can be found at your local craft and hobby store. The throat of the hook is made narrower than the rest of its body to help you work your yarn through the stitches.

Next on your hook is the shaft, probably the most important part. Most of your crocheting is done on the shaft, so its size is very important. The width of the shaft determines the hook size: the larger the size, the thicker the yarn you can use. The size is usually stamped onto the hook so that you don't have to figure it out yourself. There are three parts when you look at the stamp on a hook. First, a letter of the alphabet: these start at the letter *B* and go up. The further up the alphabet, the bigger the size of the hook. The largest hook I have ever seen in person is a *Q*. After the letter is a corresponding number. Finally, the width of the shaft is written in millimeters.

These indicators will help you identify your hook size.

Your crochet hook also has a handle, and here you have many choices. The average hook will have a straight handle that may or may not have a thumb rest indent on it. These handles are usually about four inches (10.2cm) long. But lately, since people have been known to crochet into the later years in life, ergonomic handles have been making an appearance on shelves. These handles fit into your hands better and are easier to grip. They relieve some of the stress put onto your hands and wrists while crocheting. Now, if you like to be surrounded by pretty things, you can also find hooks covered in polymer clay. These are usually artistic in nature and can be found on websites like eBay and Etsy. You can even find online tutorials to make them yourself.

Crochet hooks can be made from many different materials. I am always searching the secondhand stores looking for old hooks made from ivory or some other unique materials. Most of the hooks you will find at your local craft and hobby store are made from aluminum or plastic. Larger hooks are always plastic to help keep the weight of the hook lighter. Higher end local yarn stores will usually also carry some wonderful bamboo hooks. If you search the Internet, you will also find some amazing and beautiful hardwood hooks crafted by hand. These are my favorites, but you must remember that they are handmade and may not be the exact size needed. Because of this, I don't design with them. I do love to use mine for personal and charity items though. Last on our list of materials are steel crochet hooks. These are those small, and sometimes scary, ones you see. They are used when working with fine thread and making intricate designs. These hooks also use a different numbering and lettering system than regular yarn hooks.

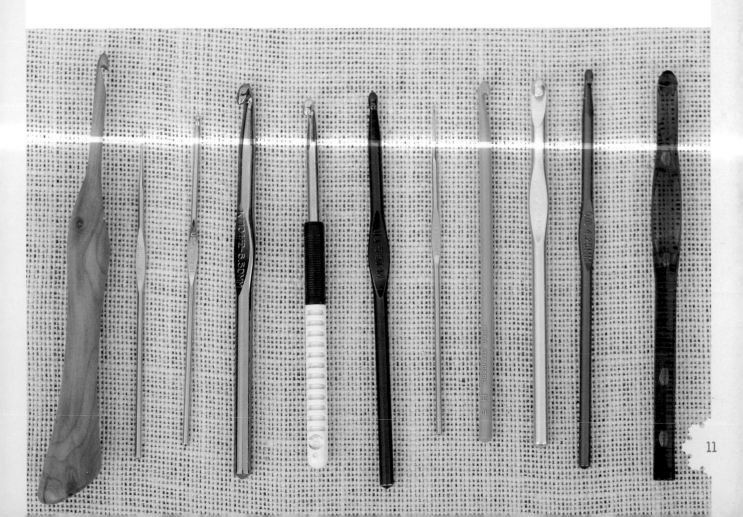

THE OTHER STUFF

You could easily go broke purchasing all the fun little accessories that go along with crocheting. But in truth, you only need a few things. All of these can be found at hobby and craft stores as well as local yarn stores. First, let's consider the necessities.

Scissors are pretty self-explanatory. I like to use a small pair of embroidery scissors because they fit into my crochet hook case. It is also nice to have a pair that folds up or has a cover to keep from possibly hurting someone. I've even seen some really neat ones that hang like a pendant on a necklace chain. The choice is yours.

A **yarn needle** or two (also known as a tapestry needle) is also a necessity. These large needles are usually pretty blunt and have a large eye that makes them easier to thread. I introduced my mother-in-law to a fabulous implement called a needle threader. She loves how much easier and faster it allows her to thread her needles.

You will also need something to measure with. I always carry a small six-inch (15.2cm) **ruler** with me. I find these great for measuring gauge, and they store nicely in my hook case and travel easily. I also keep a long fabric tape measure at home for larger items.

Stitch markers are next on my list of must-haves. These do not need to be fancy: in a pinch, you can use scraps of other yarns to mark your places. Safety pins can also stand in for stitch markers. Avoid the ones with the coils on one end because they may tangle into your project and become hard to remove. Don't use knitting stitch markers. These are usually circles that do not open and close. You need to be able to remove them! I've made my own stitch markers out of pretty beads and various findings for jewelry making such as lobster or trigger clasps and earwire or lever-backs for earrings. You can also find some beautiful ones already made online at sites such as Etsy. I've seen some great ones where the beads are numbered so that you can easily count your rows!

Last on my list of must-haves is a **pencil or pen and sticky notes**. I love to use sticky notes to mark what line I am on in a crochet pattern. Since they are sticky, you can move them to the next row as you complete a row. Also, you can make notes to yourself on them to remind you of any changes you made to a pattern.

As I mentioned before, there are a ton of accessories you can spend your money on for crocheting. I have listed the basics, but here are some other items you may want to accumulate as your finances allow.

I love a good hook case that can hold all your stuff. They can be fabric, leather or even crocheted!

A row counter is a good tool so you don't have to keep writing tally marks on your paper each time you finish a row. Also, a yarn swift and ball winder are great when you work with yarns that come to you in hanks. Lastly, a blocking board and pins are helpful when it is time to finish your items and give them a professional look.

Other items even farther down my list are things such as support gloves for your hands and wrists, pom-pom makers, yarn bobbins for colorwork, and needle gauges. These items serve a specific purpose and are needed at specific times, but they are not items you'll need as a beginner.

✳ TIPS AND TRICKS

If using yarn scraps as stitch markers, be sure that the yarn you use is light in color so it doesn't transfer any dye onto your project. You'll also want to use a smooth yarn for this, too.

yarn

There is nothing like yarn. The variety of it, the textures, and the oh-so-many colors. Some horde it, some stash it, some even actually use it—imagine that! I don't know of any crocheters who don't have different yarns stored all over their house. Or, if they are lucky, they keep their yarns organized or cataloged, and some crocheters even have their own craft rooms! (By the way, I have a craft room. Lucky me! But it IS pretty disorganized.)

Yarns can be cool or warm, silky or scratchy, machine washable or hand washable. Yarns can be puffy, silky or even flat. Thick or thin, too. Look and you will see every color under the rainbow, from amazing brights to all-natural neutrals. You can purchase yarn in long, center-pull skeins, balls and even hanks that need to be made into balls before you can work with them.

Have I mentioned that crocheters love yarn? Where would we be without it?

FIBER/CONTENT

Yarns come in many different fibers and contents. You can find plant- or animal-based natural yarns, man-made yarns and even blends of different yarns. Some of them can even be pretty exotic, too: ever hear of someone hand spinning yarn from human or cat hair? Prices can likewise vary from inexpensive to downright outrageous. Yarns have different textures and different properties. Don't be afraid to feel the yarn, snuggle the yarn and even caress the yarn. I've seen people do it! Here is a basic rundown of some yarn characteristics to help you choose what will work for you and your new crochet project.

Natural yarns are exactly what they say they are: they come from either animals or plants. There are natural yarns that can keep you cool such as cotton, hemp or linen. These yarns come from plant-derived fibers and are great for summer wearables. They can whisk away and absorb water and make good dish cloths and pot holders. Other natural yarns can keep you very, very warm. Animal fur from sheep, goats and rabbits are spun into some of the most wonderful yarns you can imagine. Examples include wool and silk. These make great hats, scarves and sweaters.

Man-made yarns are probably the most popular with crocheters. They are usually made from a petroleum product, such as plastic. Examples include acrylic and nylon yarns. These yarns are usually very sturdy, inexpensive and machine washable. Unfortunately, man-made yarns are not as warm or absorbent as natural yarns.

If you hit some of your favorite local yarn stores, you are sure to find some wonderful exotic yarns made from alpacas, angora rabbits and even yaks! But beware, most exotic yarns are on the expensive side, so choose your crochet project wisely when using them.

One of my favorite types of yarn to crochet with are fiber blends. They usually take a desirable trait from two different fibers to make the perfect blend. For example, mixing acrylic yarn with an inelastic cotton yarn produces a light yarn with stretch. These are my favorites for summer clothing. Another great combination includes mixing acrylic with wool to make a usual hand-wash-only item into something washable. You can find so many unique combinations that I couldn't even name them all. This is also a good way to keep costs of the yarns down while still being able to use some more exotic fibers.

One other type of yarn I would like to add here is recycled or repurposed yarns. Some yarn companies make Eco-friendly yarns out of recycled items like cotton fabrics and plastics. You can also make your own from old T-shirts, denim jeans, fabric and even used plastic grocery bags. I also love the idea of repurposing yarns from crocheted or knitted sweaters and blankets that you find at secondhand stores.

TEXTURE

Next to color, texture is the second most attractive attribute of yarn. Some people love to work with novelty or specialty yarns like bouclé, which features a bubbly, thick/thin texture that is usually very soft and lofty. Other people like the uniqueness of fuzzy, hair-type yarns like chenille and eyelash yarns. I remember a time when flat, tape-like yarns were very popular, but now it appears that the new trend is ruffle yarns that are easy to crochet into fashionable scarves. Of course, the most popular texture of yarn is smooth because these yarns do not pill or fuzz.

WEIGHT

The wonderful people over at the Craft Yarn Council have organized yarns into seven different standard weights and even designed cute symbols with numbers to help us identify them. These symbols help make yarn substitutions easier. Look for a picture of a skein of yarn with a number 0–6 on most kinds of yarn to figure out its "official" weight. All the projects in this book call for yarn based on these standards. The information in the chart below is taken from www.yarnstandards.com.

	LACE (0)	SUPER FINE (1)	FINE (2)	LIGHT (3)	MEDIUM (4)	BULKY (5)	SUPER BULKY (6)
WEIGHT	fingering, 10-count crochet thread	sock, fingering, 2-ply, 3-ply	sport, baby, 4-ply	light worsted, DK	worsted, afghan, aran	chunky, craft, rug	super-chunky, bulky, roving
CROCHET GAUGE RANGE*	32–42 sts	21–32 sts	16–20 sts	12–17 sts	11–14 sts	8–11 sts	5–9 sts
RECOMMENDED HOOK RANGE**	Steel*** 6, 7, 8 Regular hook B/1 (1.4mm–2.25mm)	B/1 to E/4 (2.25mm–3.5mm)	E/4 to 7 (3.5mm–4.5mm)	7 to I/9 (4.5mm–5.5mm)	I/9 to K/10½ (5.5mm–6.5mm)	K/10½ to M/13 (6.5mm–9mm)	M/13 and larger (9mm and larger)

* NOTES

* Gauge (what UK crocheters call "tension") is measured over 4" (10cm) in single crochet (except for Lace [0], which is worked in double crochet).

** US hook sizes are given first, with UK equivalents in parentheses.

*** Steel crochet hooks are sized differently from regular hooks— the higher the number, the smaller the hook, which is the reverse of regular hook sizing.

Due to everyone's unique gauge while crocheting, tension and the desired look of the finished product, suggested hook sizes are not always accurate. This chart only tells you the most common size hooks used with each yarn weight.

Let's start with **lace weight (0)**. This is the thin stuff, baby! Usually used for lacework, this yarn is also known as "fingering" weight yarn. Those scary steel hooks that I mentioned earlier are the standard sized hooks used with this weight of yarn. Don't get me wrong, I am in awe of those beautiful Irish lace pieces. This intricate type of crocheting is not for everyone, though.

Super fine wieght (1) is next on the list. Also called "sock" or "fingering" yarn, this stuff is great for socks and can make some amazing lace items. As you can see, "fingering" can be another name for both sizes 0 and 1. It is standard practice for all crochet patterns written these days to use the number system to avoid confusion.

Fine weight (2) yarn is great for making socks, lace shawls and delicate baby items. That is why it is also called "baby" and "sport" weight.

Light weight (3) yarn is probably my favorite weight of yarn. You can make a variety of items from these yarns. It makes great summer wearables along and accessories. This weight of yarn is called "DK" and "light worsted."

The most popular weight is **medium weight (4)**. Most people know this yarn as "worsted," "afghan" or "aran." These yarns can be made into just about anything you desire: bags, scarves, cozy sweaters, etc.

Appropriately named, **bulky weight (5)** yarn makes great items that you want to be thick and warm. It is also called "chunky," "craft" or "rug" yarn.

Last but not least is **super bulky weight (6)**. I think it's pretty self-explanatory, but I will add that it works up F-A-S-T! You'll also find it called "bulky" or "roving" yarn.

HOW TO READ A YARN LABEL

Again, thanks to those wonderful people over at the Craft Yarn Council, you can walk into any craft and hobby store and be able to read all about your yarn. All of the labels will have the same information. Trust me, this makes yarn shopping so much easier! Please note that yarn labels at your local yarn store may not be as complete. Many of those yarns are made in different countries, and they do not always follow the same system when identifying their yarns.

(1) Yarn name and manufacturer (usually in big, hard-to-miss letters) (not pictured).

(2) Fiber content.

(3) Yardage: tells you how much yarn is in the ball. This will be written a variety of different ways, but usually includes both standard US and metric conversions.

(4) Yarn weight: the symbol from the Craft Yarn Council that looks like a ball of yarn with a number in it. This will tell you the weight class of your yarn.

(5) Gauge information: tells you suggested hook size and approximately how many stitches are in a 4" × 4" (10.2cm × 10.2cm) swatch.

(6) Care instructions: either symbols and/or words. These are the basic standards that you find on just about anything that needs to be cleaned.

(7) Color: name, a code that goes with it, and a dye lot number.

(8) Yarn company information (not pictured).

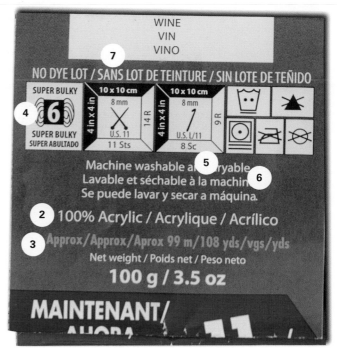

SAMPLE YARN LABEL.

✳ TIPS AND TRICKS

A word about dye lots: when buying multiple balls of yarn, check that all the balls have the same dye lot. This will ensure that the color is uniform between each ball. Some yarns will say "No Dye Lot" and you can rest assured that the colors will match.

Keep your yarn labels. If you make something for yourself, write on the label what it is. That way you'll always be able to look up the care instructions for it. Giving your finished item as a gift? Give the label, too! They'll love knowing how to take care of their precious gift.

gauge

Ask any crocheter what their least favorite part of crocheting is, and you'll have a fifty-fifty chance of hearing "Making a gauge swatch." (The other half will tell you it's weaving in ends!) As much as we dislike it, gauge is a necessary evil. If your gauge does not match the design, then your finished item has the opportunity to take on a life of its own. In the case of this book, your hat could end up fitting an elephant if your gauge is too big. Or it could end up becoming a great item to donate to your local NICU ward for premature babies.

With this book, I have tried to make the gauge process as easy as possible. Most of the designs require you to make a round gauge. You will start the hat and then, within the first few rounds, you measure your gauge. If you're lucky, you'll be spot-on at that point. If your circle is too small or big, you'll only have to rip out a few rounds (instead of the entire hat!) and change your hook. But no matter what, it is important to check your gauge.

MEASURING GAUGE IN THE ROUND

When the gauge of the pattern reads something like "First 5 rounds in pattern = 4″ (10.2cm)," this means to start working the pattern exactly as it is written. Once you complete round 5, lay your circle flat and place your ruler vertically across the top. Make sure that the ruler is centered and hitting the exact center of your circle. If your hat measures 4″ (10.2cm), your gauge is perfect and you can continue crocheting your hat. If it measures less than 4″ (10.2cm), go up a hook size or two. More than 4″ (10.2cm)? Grab a smaller hook and start again.

MEASURING GAUGE IN THE ROUND.

MEASURING GAUGE IN ROWS

When you come across a pattern where the gauge reads "10 sts and 11 rows in sc = 4" (10.2cm)," this means you will be working in rows. Unfortunately, you will have to take a few extra minutes before starting your project to make a gauge swatch. Since it reads "sc" (single crochet), you will start by chaining at least that number of stitches plus one. I usually add at least half of the original desired number because I want my gauge swatch to be bigger than the 4" (10.2cm): it is easier to measure that way. So, I would then chain 16 stitches (10 + 1 + 5). Then single crochet in the second chain from the hook and each chain across, ending with a total of 15 single crochet stitches. Chain one and then turn. Continue to work single crochet stitches in each stitch across until you have a total of about 17 rows. Once row 17 is complete, measure for gauge.

To do that, lay your swatch out flat and lay your ruler horizontally on top. You may want to mark the 0" and 4" (10.2cm) points with a straight pin or a different color of yarn. How many stitches do you have in between?

Next, you need to measure the rows. Turn your ruler vertically. Now place your pins or yarn at the 0" and 4" (10.2cm) marks, making sure the ruler aligns with the bottom of a row. How many rows do you have in between?

Do you have too many stitches and/or rows? Then go down a hook size or two. Not enough? Go up a hook size. Unfortunately, you have to create another swatch to see if your new hook size meets the required gauge. Once you meet your gauge, you are ready to move on to creating your new hat!

MEASURING GAUGE IN ROWS.

✳ TIPS AND TRICKS

What happens if your square gauge swatch meets one of the requirements, but not the other? You'll have to make a choice. Usually it's better to have the hat fit around the circumference of your head than to have the height of the hat be perfect. Make sure that your horizontal measure (number of stitches) meets the gauge requirements and use that hook.

choosing the right size

You've looked at all the beautiful photos in this book, marked your favorites, picked out some fabulous new yarns to use, plus gathered all your hooks and supplies. Now what? You need to decide what size hat to make.

HOW TO MEAUSURE FOR SIZE

You will need a few supplies. The best choice is a flexible fabric measuring tape. In a pinch, you can use a piece of nonstretchy string and a ruler or yard stick. It's also a good idea to have someone to help you. If not, you'll need to stand in front of a mirror. Now take your measuring tape and, without twisting it, wrap it around your head where you would normally have a hat sit. That's approximately at the top of your ears. Be sure to keep the tape measure level to the ground. Take a look and see where the ends meet. That's your head circumference. If you happen to fall in between whole numbers, choose the one you think will work best for you. I would suggest the larger size unless the design features a very stretchy brim. Now you know your head circumference and can use that number to pick the right hat size.

HAT SIZES IN THIS BOOK

In this book, I created my own hat size charts. With my many years of experience designing crocheted hats, I have unfortunately found that the guidelines for standard sizes are not accurate. Not everyone's head is the same size at the same times in their lives. Some families have larger heads, some have smaller. My family, for instance, has smaller heads. Also, you sometimes have to take into consideration the amount of hair on a person's head. I've seen some little girls with long, thick hair that adds to their head circumference. I also put the sizes closer together so that you can create a better fit for your size. In general, this is the guideline used:

	SMALL	MEDIUM	LARGE
GIRLS'	18" (45.7cm)	19" (48.3cm)	20" (50.8cm)
BOYS'	19" (48.3cm)	20" (50.3cm)	21" (53.3cm)
WOMEN'S	21" (53.3cm)	22" (55.9cm)	23" (58.4cm)
MEN'S	22" (55.9cm)	23" (58.4cm)	24" (61cm)

✳ TIPS AND TRICKS

Once you know what size you are making, I suggest grabbing a pen or highlighter and marking all the specific numbers, rows, and directions for your size. It will help keep you from getting confused.

finishing techniques

You've worked so hard on your new hat and are so excited with how it turned out! But now what? It doesn't look exactly like the pictures. You have yarn ends sticking out everywhere, and it's probably missing something. It is time to finish your crochet project. Let's go over some of the basics that you'll be using. Each pattern will have a section called "Finishing" to help guide you through this process.

WEAVING IN ENDS

This is something you almost always have to do, no matter what your crochet project. It's really simple, but it can be tedious, especially on projects that use multiple colors.

First, thread your yarn needle with one of the loose tail ends, and turn your work to the wrong side. Remember, your goal here is to make the ends disappear. Next, weave the threaded needle through the crochet piece in a back and forth direction, being sure to follow the path of the stitches and not go diagonally. Do this a few times, for approximately 2"–3" (5.1cm–7.6cm) of the tail, and then snip it off close to your work. Continue with the remaining ends until all ends are woven in. Whenever possible, try to weave the ends into a section of the same color. (Note: contrasting yarn was used in the photo for clarity.)

WEAVING IN ENDS.

FRINGE

Fringe is one of the easiest ways to dress up your finished project. Once you choose which yarn(s) you will be using, wrap it over and over again around something sturdy, about 2" (5.1cm) longer than the desired length of your fringe. Things I like to use include CD cases, DVD cases, cardboard and hardback books. Once you've wrapped your heart out, or at least counted approximately how many pieces of fringe you will need, it's time to cut the yarn along one edge and from the skein of yarn. Now you're ready to make fringe!

how to make fringe

1 Gather your strands of yarn and fold them in half. Insert a large crochet hook along the edge of your work, and hook the strands at the fold and pull a loop partially through.

2 Using the crochet hook or your fingers, pull the loose ends of the yarn through the loop.

3 Finish the fringe by pulling snugly to secure. Once you finish all the fringe, trim it to an even length.

TASSELS

Tassels are another way to dress up your finished pieces. Think of them as fancy fringe. Once more, you'll need a sturdy item to wrap your yarn around, and again, it should be about 1"–2" (2.5cm–5.1cm) longer than you want your desired tassel. Wrap your yarn around this object many times until it is about ¼" (6mm) thick. Cut the yarn from the skein and then cut another piece of yarn around 8" (20.3cm) long. Thread that separate piece of yarn under all the strands you have wrapped and tie it tightly with a knot. Then, cut the yarn off the object at the opposite end of your knot. Once free, you'll wrap the long ends tightly around the folded top of the tassel about ½" (13mm) down, then thread a needle with the long ends and stick it through the head of the tassel. This will become the part that gets attached to your crochet piece. Trim the ends evenly and you are done.

POM-POMS

I can't think of a cuter finishing touch than a pom-pom! You'll find them on a number of designs in this book. Making them is not as easy as it looks, however. Your first option when making pom-poms is to use a pom-pom maker that you can purchase at your local craft and hobby store. All you have to do is follow the directions that come with it. But if that is not an option, pom-poms can be made using two pieces of cardboard. You'll need two large circles of cardboard a little larger than your desired pom-pom size. They also need to have a hole cut out of the center that should be half the size of the circle—essentially two cardboard donuts. Cut a small section out of the donuts, which will make them look like *C*'s.

Now that you have your pom-pom maker, follow the directions on the next page to make your pom-pom.

How to Make a Pom-Pom

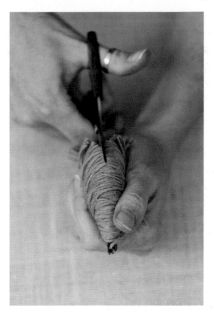

1 Holding the cardboard pieces together, wrap your yarn around the length of the cardboard. Continue to wrap until the center hole is full. This makes a nice and fluffy pom-pom. Once you are finished, cut the yarn from the skein and cut another long piece of yarn.

2 Carefully cut the loops of yarn along the outside edge of your cardboard.

3 Place your long strand between the two pieces of cardboard. Tie this piece of yarn very tightly, then remove the cardboard pieces.

4 Fluff your pom-pom and give it a nice trim to make it look pretty. You'll need to leave the two ends that you tied around the center long so that you can attach the pom-pom to your work.

✳ TIPS AND TRICKS

When tying the center of your pom-pom, try using dental floss instead of another piece of yarn. You are able to make a very tight and secure knot from it.

BRAIDS

Think of braids as fancy, long fringe. Most of the time, you will only have to measure and cut the yarn using a ruler or tape measure as your guide. The pattern will tell you how long to cut the strands. When it is time to join the braids, you will attach them the same way that you attach fringe. Once that is done, then you will separate the strands into three sections according to the pattern directions. Now braid. Once you have about 4" (10.2cm) of yarn left, securely tie the braid with an overhand knot and trim the ends evenly. Repeat for the second side.

APPLIQUÉ

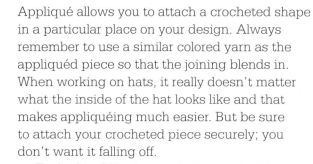

Appliqué allows you to attach a crocheted shape in a particular place on your design. Always remember to use a similar colored yarn as the appliquéd piece so that the joining blends in. When working on hats, it really doesn't matter what the inside of the hat looks like and that makes appliquéing much easier. But be sure to attach your crocheted piece securely; you don't want it falling off.

To do this, I like to use the long tail of the appliqué piece. Place your appliqué where desired on the item and pin it in place. Threading the long tail through your needle, work your way around the perimeter of the item from right side to wrong side and back to right side. Do this at short intervals until you get all around the item. Finish with the tail on the wrong side and weave in your ends. Remove your pins and you are done.

✳ TIPS AND TRICKS

I like to count how many times I go over the center section so that I can try to make each braid the same length.

RUNNING STITCH

The running stitch is used to gather or close your work. You'll see it used in a few of the designs in this book. To make a running stitch, you will create straight stitches. First, pass the threaded needle over the right side of the work and then back to the wrong side at desired intervals. You are basically forming dashed lines. These stitches can be worked in equal or varying lengths, horizontally, vertically, or diagonally as stated in the design.

BLOCKING

Blocking your finished item has a lot of positive benefits. It gives your item a professional look and will help with any curling edges. Hats do not usually need to be blocked unless there is a specific look you want to achieve. Scarves will look better when blocked.

To do this, I use a clean spray bottle full of water, a blocking board and straight pins. For a scarf, spread it out over the blocking board until you get the desired look and size. Put the pins around the edges and/or center to keep it in place. Now, spray it with the water until damp and allow to dry. Once dry, remove the pins and it should be ready.

If you want to block a hat, first spray it down with the water. Then place it over a head form or mannequin to dry.

✳ **TIPS AND TRICKS**

Don't have a blocking board? You can always lay items on a thick towel.

CHAPTER ONE

girls' hats

Girls' hats are probably my favorite accessory to design. I have so much fun creating the designs and imagining the little girl's face when she sees a hat that perfectly suits her personality. Of course, I am biased since I have my very own little girl to dress up (although she is not so little anymore!). Every girl should have an adorable hat or two in their wardrobe: think of all the oohs and ahhs she will receive while she is out and about.

paw prints

SKILL LEVEL: EASY

Hands down, this is my daughter's favorite design in the book, but any kitten lover will purr with delight when she sees this hat. With a built-in scarf and mittenlike pockets, an adorable bow and fun paw prints, it is no wonder that this hat is a favorite.

Yarn

Bernat Bamboo (86% viscose from bamboo, 12% acrylic, 2% polyester; 63 yds/57m per 2.1 oz/60g ball) or similar bulky weight yarn in color #92316 Easter (MC), 5 (6) skeins

Bernat Satin (100% acrylic: 200 yds/182m per 3.5 oz/100g ball) in color #04307 Sultana (CC), 1 skein

Hooks and Notions

Size US K/10.5 (6.5mm) crochet hook or size needed to obtain gauge

Size US F/5 (3.75mm) crochet hook or size needed to obtain gauge

Stitch marker

Yarn needle

Finished Measurements

Girls' S/M (Girls' M/L)

17" (43.1cm) (19" [48.3cm])

Gauge

10 sts and 9 rows in hdc = 4" (10.2cm)

✳ SPECIAL STITCHES

Magic Loop technique: See Stitch Glossary for details.

✳ PATTERN NOTES

Ch 1 at beg of row does not count as a hdc.

Make ch 1 at beg of row loosely and pull to the height of a hdc.

Hat is worked flat and seamed to get its shape.

The hood is very forgiving in size, but to get a perfect fit with the scarf, measure from the center of the neck to the wrist and create the scarf, rows 19 (21) to 56 (60), to that length.

CROCHET THE HAT

Hood + First Side

Row 1 (RS): Using the larger hook and MC, leave a long tail for seaming and ch 41 (51); hdc in second ch from hook and each ch across. Turn. (40 [50] sc)

Rows 2–18 (2–20): Ch 1; hdc in each st across. Turn.

Row 19 (21): Ch 1; hdc in first 16 (18) sts. Turn. (16 [18] hdc)

Row 20 (22): Ch 1; hdc in each st across. Turn.

Row 21 (23): Ch 1; hdc dec over first 2 sts, hdc in next 12 (14) sts, hdc dec over last 2 sts. Turn. (14 [16] hdc)

Rows 22–56 (24–60): Rep Row 20 (22).

Row 57 (61): Ch 1; hdc dec over first 2 sts, hdc in next 10 (12) sts, hdc dec over last 2 sts. Turn. (12 [14] hdc)

Row 58 (62): Ch 1; hdc dec over first 2 sts, hdc in next 8 (10) sts, hdc dec over last 2 sts. Turn. (10 [12] hdc)

Row 59 (63): Rep Row 20 (22).

Row 60 (64): Ch 1; 2 hdc in first st, hdc in next 8 (10) sts, 2 hdc in last st. Turn. (12 [14] hdc)

Row 61 (65): Ch 1; 2 hdc in first st, hdc in next 10 (12) sts, 2 hdc in last st. Turn. (14 [16] hdc)

Rows 62–81 (66–85): Rep Row 20 (22).

Rows 82–83 (86–87): Rep Rows 57 and 58 (61 and 62). Finish off leaving a long tail for seaming.

Second Side

With WS facing, sk next 8 (14) sts on Row 20 (22). Join MC with a sl st to next st. Hdc in same st as joining and next 15 (17) sts. Turn. (16 [18] hdc)

Rep Rows 21–83 (23–87) of first side.

Ears (make 2)

Rnd 1: Starting with larger hook, MC, and magic lp technique, ch 1; 4 sc in loop. Do not join. Use stitch marker to mark beg of rnd. (4 sc)

Rnd 2: 2 sc in each st. (8 sc)

Rnd 3: Sc in each sc around.

Rnd 4: [Sc in first 3 sts, 2 sc in next st] 2 times. (10 sc)

Rnd 5: [Sc in first 4 sts, 2 sc in next st] 2 times. (12 sc)

Rnd 6: [Sc in first 2 sts, 2 sc in next st] 4 times. (16 sc)

Rnd 7: Sc in each sc around. Join with a sl st to first sc. Finish off leaving a long tail for sewing.

Bow

Row 1: With smaller hook and CC, ch 31. Sc in second ch from hook and each ch across. Ch 1, turn. (30 sc)

Rows 2–6: Sc in each sc across. Ch 1, turn.

Row 7: Sc in each sc across. Ch 1, fold in half horizontally and sl st row ends together. Finish off leaving a long tail for bow center.

Centering the seam to the back, wrap the long tail multiple times around the center to form a bow. Tack to secure and finish off.

Trim (for hood)

With CC, RS facing, and smaller hook, attach yarn with a sl st to end of Row 20. Sc in same sp as joining, [5 dc, sc in next row end] 18 times, evenly placing sts along row edge to Row 20 of other side, ending with a sc in next row and finish off.

Paw Prints Toes (make 8)

With smaller hook, CC, and magic lp technique, (sc, hdc, 2 dc, hdc, sc, hdc, 2 dc, hdc) in ring. Join with a sl st to first sc. Finish off leaving a long tail for sewing.

Paw Print Center (make 2)

Row 1: With smaller hook, CC, and magic lp technique, 12 dc in ring. Join with a sl st to first dc.

Row 2: Ch 2, 2 dc in each st around. Join with a sl st to first dc. (24 dc)

Row 3: Ch 1, sc in same st as joining, hdc in next st, [2 dc in next st] 2 times, hdc in next st, sc in next 4 sts. 2 hdc in next st, 2 dc in next st, dc in next st, 2 dc in next st, hdc in next st, sc in next 2 sts. Hdc in next st, 2 dc in next,

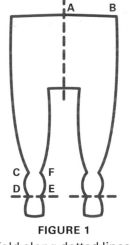

FIGURE 1
Fold along dotted lines.

dc in next st, 2 dc in next st, 2 hdc in next st, sc in last 3 sts. Join with a sl st to first sc. Finish off leaving a long tail for sewing.

Finishing

Fold in half with RS facing and seam from point A to point B. Fold mittens up with WS facing and seam from point D to point C, and again from point E to point F, leaving an opening at the top for hands (Figure 1). Sew ears onto hat where desired. Sew bow to front of ear. Sew paw prints onto mittens.

pixie bonnet

SKILL LEVEL: EASY

This design is perfect for the little pixie, sprite or fairy in your life. I adore the pointed accent at the crown and the bonnetlike shape. The flowers add a whimsical finishing touch and the colors will match just about anything. Be sure to pay close attention to the directions when working the back of the hat; its construction is a little different than most.

Yarn

Cascade Yarns 220 Superwash Sport (100% superwash merino wool; 136 yds/125m per 1.75 oz/50g ball) or similar light weight yarn in colors:

- no. 817 Aran (MC), 1 skein
- no. 820 Lemon (CC1), 1 skein
- no. 827 Coral (CC2), 1 skein

Hooks and Notions

Size US G/6 (4mm) crochet hook or size needed to obtain gauge

Stitch markers

Yarn needle

Finished Measurements

Girls' S (Girls' M, Girls' L):

18" (45.7cm) (19" [48.3cm], 20" [50.8cm])

Gauge

First 14 rnds in pattern = 4" (10.2cm)

✳ SPECIAL STITCHES

Herringbone Half Double Crochet (hhdc): See Stitch Glossary for details.

Magic Loop technique: See Stitch Glossary for details.

✳ PATTERN NOTES

When measuring for gauge, allow hat to keep shape. It will not be flat.

Hat is worked in the rnd, from the top down.

Do not join at the end of each row. Use a st marker to locate rnd beg.

CROCHET THE HAT

Rnd 1 (RS): Starting with MC and magic lp technique, ch 1; 6 sc in lp.

Rnds 2–3: Hhdc in each st around. (6 hhdc)

Rnd 4: 2 hhdc in each st around. (12 hhdc)

Rnds 5–6: Hhdc in each st around.

Rnd 7: *2 hhdc in next st, hhdc in next st. Rep from * around. (18 hhdc)

Rnd 8: Hhdc in each st around.

Rnd 9: *2 hhdc in next st, hhdc in next 2 sts. Rep from * around. (24 hhdc)

Rnd 10: Hhdc in each st around.

Rnd 11: *2 hhdc in next st, hhdc in next 3 sts. Rep from * around. (30 hhdc)

Rnd 12: *2 hhdc in next st, hhdc in next 4 sts. Rep from * around. (36 hhdc)

Rnd 13: *2 hhdc in next st, hhdc in next 5 sts. Rep from * around. (42 hhdc)

Rnd 14: *2 hhdc in next st, hhdc in next 6 sts. Rep from * around. (48 hhdc)

Rnd 15: *2 hhdc in next st, hhdc in next 7 sts. Rep from * around. (54 hhdc)

Rnd 16: *2 hhdc in next st, hhdc in next 8 sts. Rep from * around. (60 hhdc)

Rnd 17: *2 hhdc in next st, hhdc in next 9 sts. Rep from * around. (66 hhdc)

SIZE M AND L

Rnd 18: *2 hhdc in next st, hhdc in next 10 sts. Rep from * around. (72 hhdc)

SIZE L

Rnd 19: *2 hhdc in next st, hhdc in next 11 sts. Rep from * around. (78 hhdc)

ALL SIZES

Rnds 18–23 (19–25, 20–27): Hhdc in each st around.

Round 24 (26, 28): Hhdc in first 10 sts, sc in next st, sl st in next 6 sts, sc in next st, hhdc around.

Rnd 25 (27, 29): Hhdc in first 8 sts, sc in next st, sl st in next st, sl st in BL of next 8 sts, sl st in next st, sc in next st, hhdc around.

Rnd 26 (28, 30): Hhdc in first 6 sts, sc in next st, sl st in next st, sl st in BL of next 12 sts, sl st in next st, sc in next st, hhdc around.

Rnd 27 (29, 31): Hhdc in first 4 sts, sc in next st, sl st in next st, sl st in BL of next 16 sts, sl st in next st, sc in next st, hhdc around.

Rnd 28 (30, 32): Hhdc in first 2 sts, sc in next st, sl st in next st, sl st in BL of next 20 sts, sl st in next st, sc in next st, hhdc around.

Rnd 29 (31, 33): Sc in first st, sl st in next st, sl st in BL of next 24 sts, sl st in next st. Fasten off. Mark center 50 sts on front. You will now begin working in rows.

Brim

ALL SIZES

Row 1: Attach CC1 with a sl st to first st. Ch 1, sc in same st as joining and next 49 sts. Sl st in next st. Turn. (50sc)

Row 2: Sk sl st, sc in each sc across. Change to MC, turn. (50 sc)

Row 3: Ch 1; sc in first st, [sk 1 st, 5 dc in next st, sk next st, sc in next st] 12 times. Turn. (12 shells)

Row 4: Sk sc, sl st in next 3 dc, ch 1, sc in same st, [5 dc in next sc, sk 2 dc, sc in next dc] 11 times. Turn. (11 shells)

Row 5: Sk sc, sl st in next 3 dc, ch 1, sc in same st, [5 dc in next sc, sk 2 dc, sc in next dc] 10 times. Fasten off. (10 shells)

Row 6: With RS facing, attach CC2 with a sl st to same st as Row 1. Sl st in each st across until you reach other end of shells. Finish off.

Rnd 1: With CC1 and magic lp technique, ch 1; 6 sc in ring. Join with a sl st and CC2 to BL of first sc.

Rnd 2: (Ch 2, 2 dc, ch 2, sl st) in BL of each st around. Join with a sl st to same st as joining. Fasten off leaving a long tail for sewing.

Finishing

Weave in ends. Sew flowers on brim Row 1.

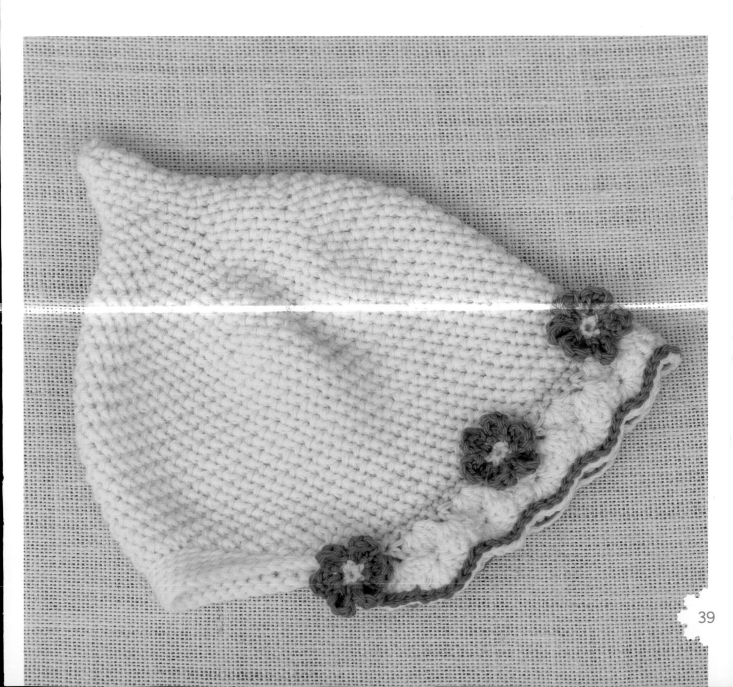

her majesty

D o you have a little princess? Then she needs this hat. It features a simple design with a fold-up brim and stunning crown accent. It will work up quickly and put a smile on her face, too. For best results, add a little fabric stiffener to the crown part and block it to help hold its shape.

Yarn

Lion Brand Vanna's Choice (100% acrylic; 170 yds/156m per 3.5 oz/100g ball) or similar medium weight yarn in color no. 860-101 Pink (MC), 1 skein

Lion Brand Vanna's Glamour (96% acrylic, 4% metallic polyester; 202 yds/185m per 1.75 oz/50g ball) or similar fine weight yarn in color no. 861-170 Topaz (CC), 1 skein

Hooks and Notions

Size US J/10 (6mm) crochet hook or size needed to obtain gauge

Size US F/5 (3.75mm) crochet hook or size needed to obtain gauge

Fabric stiffener (optional)

Yarn needle

Finished Measurements

Girls' S (Girls' M, Girls' L):

18" (45.7cm) (19" [48.3cm], 20" [50.8cm])

Gauge

First 12 rnds in pattern = 4" (10.2cm)

✳ SPECIAL STITCHES

Magic Loop technique: See Stitch Glossary for details.

✳ PATTERN NOTES

First st of each rnd is worked into the same st as joining.

Hat is worked from the top down.

Hat is worked in front loops (FL) only unless pattern states otherwise. Trim is worked through both lps.

41

CROCHET THE HAT

Rnd 1 (RS): Starting with larger hook, MC and magic lp technique, ch 1; 6 sc in lp. Join with a sl st to first sc. (6 sc)

Rnd 2: Ch 1, 2 sc in each sc around. Join with a sl st to first sc. (12 sc)

Rnd 3: Ch 1; *sc in first st, 2 sc in next st. Rep from * around. Join with a sl st to first sc. (18 sc)

Rnd 4: Ch 1; *sc in first 2 sts, 2 sc in next st. Rep from * around. Join with a sl st to first sc. (24 sc)

Rnd 5: Ch 1; *sc in first 3 sts, 2 sc in next st. Rep from * around. Join with a sl st to first sc. (30 sc)

Rnd 6: Ch 1; *sc in first 4 sts, 2 sc in next st. Rep from * around. Join with a sl st to first sc. (36 sc)

Rnd 7: Ch 1; *sc in first 5 sts, 2 sc in next st. Rep from * around. Join with a sl st to first sc. (42 sc)

Rnd 8: Ch 1; *sc in first 6 sts, 2 sc in next st. Rep from * around. Join with a sl st to first sc. (48 sc)

SIZE M AND L
Rnd 9: Ch 1; *sc in first 7 sts, 2 sc in next st. Rep from * around. Join with a sl st to first sc. (54 sc)

SIZE L
Rnd 10: Ch 1; *sc in first 8 sts, 2 sc in next st. Rep from * around. Join with a sl st to first sc. (60 sc)

ALL SIZES
Rnds 9–24 (10–25, 11–26): Ch 1; sc in each st around. Join with a sl st to first sc. (48 [54, 60] sc)

Rnd 25 (26, 27): Ch 1; sc in each st around. Join with a sl st to first sc. Finish off.

Trim

Rnd 1: Turn hat inside out with WS facing. With CC1 and smaller hook, attach yarn with a sl st to any st in Rnd 25 (26, 27). 2 sc in same st as joining and each st around. Join with a sl st to first sc. (96 [108, 120] sc)

Rnd 2: Ch 1; sc in each st around. Join with a sl st to first sc.

Rnd 3: Ch 1; sc in first 3 sc, *ch 2, sk next st, sc in next 5 sts. Rep from * around ending last rep with sc in last 2 sts. Join with a sl st to first sc.

Rnd 4: Ch 1; sc in first st, *(3 dc, ch 5, 3 dc) in ch-2 sp, sk 2 sc, sc in next sc. Rep from * around. Join with a sl st to first sc.

Rnd 5: Ch 1; sc3tog in first 3 sts, sc in next st *(sc, ch 3, 2 sc, ch 5, 2 sc, ch 3, sc) in ch-5 sp. Sc in next sc, sc5tog over next 5 sts, sc in next st. Rep from * around. Finish with sc3tog in last 3 sts and join with a sl st to first sc. Finish off.

Finishing

Weave in ends. Fold hat with RS facing and fold brim up to wear. If desired, block and use fabric stiffener on crown trim.

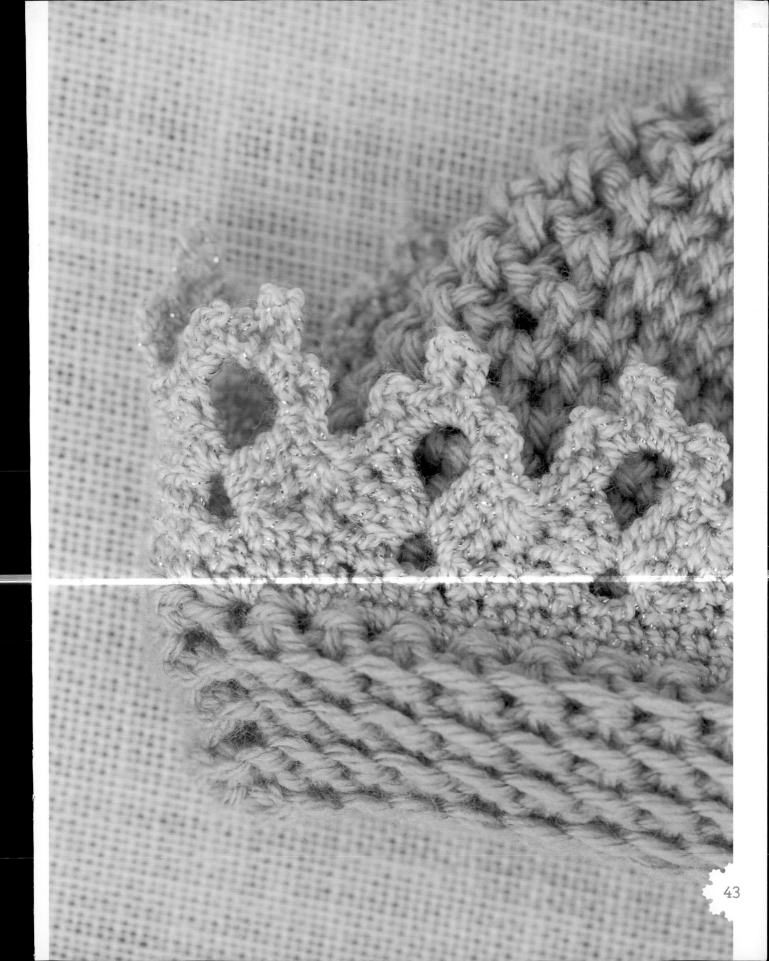

rainbow set

SKILL LEVEL: EASY

This versatile set features an amazingly beautiful, self-rainbowing yarn and fun pom-poms. The design is simple to create but has lots of options when wearing. The hat can be worn folded up and snug to the head and can even be made with or without a ponytail hole for girls with long hair. The hat can also be unfolded and worn slouchy. The simple scarf features a keyhole to weave the loose end though or simply tie it around the neck.

Yarn

Cascade Yarns Casablanca (60% wool, 20% silk, 20% mohair; 220 yds/200m per 3.5 oz/100g ball) or similar medium weight yarn in color no. 11 Rainbow, 4 skeins

Hooks and Notions

Size US H/8 (5mm) crochet hook or size needed to obtain gauge

Yarn needle

Finished Measurements

Hat: Girls' S (Girls' M, Girls' L):

18" (45.7cm) (19" [48.3cm], 20" [50.8cm])

Scarf: one size

5" × 46" (12.7cm × 116.8cm)

Gauge

15 sts and 10 rows in pattern = 4" (10.2cm)

✳ PATTERN NOTES

Hat is worked flat in rows then seamed and gathered at top.

Hat is worked in back loops (BL) only unless pattern states otherwise.

When starting the second skein of yarn, you may want to start with the similar color in coloring sequence to keep the rainbow colors in pattern.

45

CROCHET THE HAT

Row 1 (RS): Loosely ch 49 (51, 53); working in back hump of ch, sc in second ch from hook, dc in next ch. *Sc in next ch, dc in next. Rep from * across. Turn.

Row 2: Ch 1; working in BL, sc in first st, dc in next st. *Sc in next st, dc in next. Rep from * across. Turn.

Rows 3–40 (3–42, 3–44): Rep Row 2. Finish off leaving a long tail for seaming.

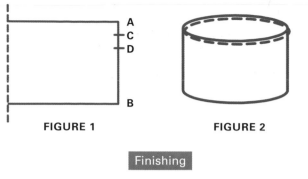

FIGURE 1   FIGURE 2

Finishing

Fold hat with RS facing and use long tail to seam first row to last (from point A to point B) (figure 1). For optional ponytail opening, leave a 2" (5.1cm) hole in seaming approximately 2½" (6.4cm) from crown (from point C to point D). Seam along crown edge with running st and pull tightly to close (figure 2). Make a large pom-pom and attach to crown top. Weave in all ends.

CROCHET THE SCARF

Row 1 (RS): Leaving a long tail, loosely ch 175; working in back hump of ch, sc in second ch from hook, dc in next ch. *Sc in next ch, dc in next. Rep from * across. Turn.

Row 2: Ch 1; working in BL, sc in first st, dc in next st. *Sc in next st, dc in next. Rep from * across. Turn.

Rows 3–6: Rep Row 2.

Row 7: Ch 1; working in BL, sc in first st, dc in next st. [Sc in next st, dc in next] 20 times. Ch 16, sk next 16 sts, *sc in next st, dc in next. Rep from * across. Turn.

Row 8: Ch 1; working in BL, sc in first st, dc in next st. *Sc in next st, dc in next. Rep from * across working in all sts and chs. Turn.

Rows 9–12: Rep Row 2. Finish off leaving a long tail.

Finishing

Using a running st, sew yarn ends through each scarf end edge and pull tightly to gather. Make 2 large pom-poms and attach to scarf ends. Weave in all ends.

CHAPTER TWO

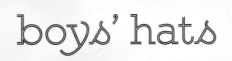

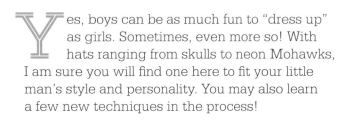

Yes, boys can be as much fun to "dress up" as girls. Sometimes, even more so! With hats ranging from skulls to neon Mohawks, I am sure you will find one here to fit your little man's style and personality. You may also learn a few new techniques in the process!

grand valley

Dressed up or dressed down, this dapper hat is sure to make your young man ready for any occasion. If you've never tried a cluster stitch before, I encourage you to try it now. The stitch is relatively easy, and the finished product is well worth the extra effort.

Yarn

Cascade Yarns Greenland (100% merino wool superwash; 137 yds/125m per 3.5 oz/100g ball) or similar medium weight yarn in colors:

> no. 3546 Indigo Heather (MC), 2 skeins

> no. 3501 Natural (CC), 1 skein

Bernat Satin (100% acrylic: 200 yds/182m per 3.5 oz/ 100g ball) in color no. 04307 Sultana (CC), 1 skein

Hooks and Notions

Size US J/10 (6mm) crochet hook or size needed to obtain gauge

Size US G/7 (4.5mm) crochet hook or size needed to obtain gauge

Yarn needle

Finished Measurements

Boys' S (Boys' M, Boys' L)

19" (48.3cm) (20" [50.8cm], 21" [53.3cm])

Gauge

First 8 rnds in pattern = 4" (10.2cm)

✳ SPECIAL STITCHES

Cluster (CL): See Stitch Glossary for details.

Magic Loop technique: See Stitch Glossary for details.

CROCHET THE HAT

Rnd 1 (RS): Starting with MC, larger hook and magic loop technique, ch 3 (counts as first dc); 11 dc in ring. Join with a sl st to first dc. (12 dc)

Rnd 2: Ch 3 (counts as first dc), dc in same st as joining and 2 dc in each st around. Join with a sl st to first dc. (24 dc)

Rnd 3: Ch 2, *sk next st, CL in next st. Working in front of CL just made, CL in skipped st (crossed CL made). Dc in same st as first CL. Rep from * around. Join with a sl st to first crossed CL. (12 crossed CL and 12 dc)

Rnd 4: Ch 1; 2 sc in same st as joining, sc in next 4 sts. *2 sc in next st, sc in next 4 sts. Rep from * around. Join with a sl st to first sc. (42 sc)

Rnd 5: Rep Rnd 3. (21 crossed CL and 21 dc)

Rnd 6: Ch 1; sc in same st as joining and each st around. Join with a sl st to first sc. (63 sc)

Rnd 7: Ch 2, *sk next st, CL in next st. Working in front of CL just made, CL in skipped st (crossed CL made). Dc in next st. Rep from * around. Join with a sl st to first crossed CL. (21 crossed CL and 21 dc)

Rnds 8–13: Rep Rnds 6 and 7.

Rnd 14: Rep Rnd 6.

SIZE S

Rnd 15: Ch 1; sc in same st as joining and next 3 sts, [sc dec over next 2 sts, sc in next 4 sts] 9 times. Sc dec over next 2 sts, sc in last 3 sts. Join CC1 with a sl st to first sc. (53 sc)

Rnd 16: Loosely ch 1; hdc in same st as joining and each st around. Join MC with a sl st to first hdc.

Rnd 17: Rep Rnd 16. Fasten off.

SIZE M

Rnd 15: Ch 1; sc in same st as joining and next 9 sts, [sc dec over next 2 sts, sc in next 10 sts] 4 times. Sc dec over next 2 sts, sc in last 3 sts. Join CC1 with a sl st to first sc. (58 sc)

Rnd 16: Loosely ch 1; hdc in same st as joining and each st around. Join MC with a sl st to first hdc.

Rnd 17: Rep Rnd 6.

Rnd 18: Rep Rnd 17. Fasten off.

SIZE L

Rnds 15–16: Rep Rnd 6. Join CC1 with a sl st to first sc. (63 sc)

Rnd 17: Loosely ch 1; hdc in same st as joining and each st around. Join MC with a sl st to first hdc.

Rnd 18: Rep Rnd 6.

Rnd 19: Rep Rnd 17. Fasten off.

Brim

ALL SIZES

Row 1: With smaller hook and MC, sk next 23 sts on Rnd 17 (18, 19), attach yarn with a sl st to the 24th st. Ch 1; Fphdc around same st as joining and next 15 (16, 17) sts. Sl st in next 2 sts of hat Rnd 17 (18, 19). Turn. (16 [17, 18] fphdc)

Row 2: 2 hdc in first st of brim, hdc in next 14 (15, 16) sts, 2 hdc in last st of brim. Sl st in next 2 sts of hat band Rnd 17 (18, 19). Turn. (18 [19, 20] hdc)

Row 3: 3 hdc in first st of brim, hdc in next 16 (17, 18) sts, 3 hdc in last st of brim. Sl st in next 2 sts of hat band Rnd 17 (18, 19). Turn. (22 [23, 24] hdc)

Row 4: 3 hdc in first st of brim, hdc in next 20 (21, 22) sts, 3 hdc in next st. Sl st in next 2 sts of hat band Rnd 17 (18, 19). Turn. (26 [27, 28] hdc)

Row 5: 3 hdc in first st of brim, 2 hdc in next st, hdc in next 22 (23, 24) sts, 2 hdc in next st, 3 hdc in last st. Join with a sl st to next st of hat band Rnd 17 (18, 19). Finish off. (32 [33, 34] hdc)

With larger hook, attach MC with a sl st to any st on hat Rnd 17 (18, 19). Ch 1; sc in each st around hat and brim. Finish off.

Weave in ends. If needed, block the brim to desired shape.

shredder

Many little boys dream of having a Mohawk at times, but not too many moms are willing. So, why not compromise with this fun-loving design? The construction is simple, but the fringe Mohawk may take a little time and concentration.

Yarn

Plymouth Yarn Encore Worsted (75% acrylic, 25% wool; 200 yds/183m per 3.5 oz/100g ball) or similar medium weight yarn in colors:

> no. 1415 Fawn Mix (MC), 1 skein
>
> no. 0479 Neon Orange (CC1), 1 skein
>
> no. 0477 Neon Green (CC2), 1 skein
>
> no. 0476 Neon Yellow (CC3); 1 skein

Hooks and Notions

Size US J/10 (6mm) crochet hook or size needed to obtain gauge

Yarn needle

Finished Measurements

Boys' S (Boys' M, Boys' L):

19" (48.3cm) (20" [50.8cm], 21" [53.3cm])

Gauge

First 8 rnds in pattern = 4½" (11.4cm)

❋ SPECIAL STITCHES

Magic Loop technique: See Stitch Glossary for details.

❋ PATTERN NOTES

First st of each rnd is worked in the same st as joining.

Ch 1 at beg of each hdc rnd is worked loosely to the height of a hdc and does not count as a st.

57

CROCHET THE HAT

Rnd 1: Starting with MC and magic lp technique, ch 1; 8 hdc in lp. Join with a sl st to first hdc. (8 hdc)

Rnd 2: Ch 1; 2 hdc in each st around. Join with a sl st to first hdc. (16 hdc)

Rnd 3: Ch 1; *hdc in first st, 2 hdc in next st. Rep from * around. Join with a sl st to first hdc. (24 hdc)

Rnd 4: Ch 1; *hdc in first 2 sts, 2 hdc in next st. Rep from * around. Join with a sl st to first hdc. (32 hdc)

Rnd 5: Ch 1; *hdc in first 3 sts, 2 hdc in next st. Rep from * around. Join with a sl st to first hdc. (40 hdc)

Rnd 6: Ch 1; *hdc in first 4 sts, 2 hdc in next st. Rep from * around. Join with a sl st to first hdc. (48 hdc)

SIZE M AND L
Rnd 7: Ch 1; *hdc in first 5 sts, 2 hdc in next st. Rep from * around. Join with a sl st to first hdc. (56 hdc)

SIZE L
Rnd 8: Ch 1; *hdc in first 6 sts, 2 hdc in next st. Rep from * around. Join with a sl st to first hdc. (64 hdc)

ALL SIZES
Rnds 7–14 (8–15, 9–16): Ch 1; hdc in each st around. Join with a sl st to first hdc. (48 [56, 64] hdc)

Rnd 15 (16, 17): Ch 1; *Fpdc around first st, bpdc around next. Rep from * around. Join with a sl st to first fpdc.

Rnd 16 (17, 18): Ch 1; *Fpdc around first fpdc, bpdc around next bpdc. Rep from * around. Join with a sl st to the first fpdc. Finish off.

Finishing

Weave in ends. Cut numerous pieces of CC1, CC2 and CC3 yarns that are approximately 8" (20.3cm) long. Attach CC yarns as desired to hat using fringe method then tie in an overhand knot to secure. Separate each yarn end into 3 sections each and trim to desired lengths. Sample has rows of 2 neon yellow, 2 neon orange, and 2 neon green trimmed to 1" (2.5cm) in front and gradually getting longer to 3" (7.6cm) in the back.

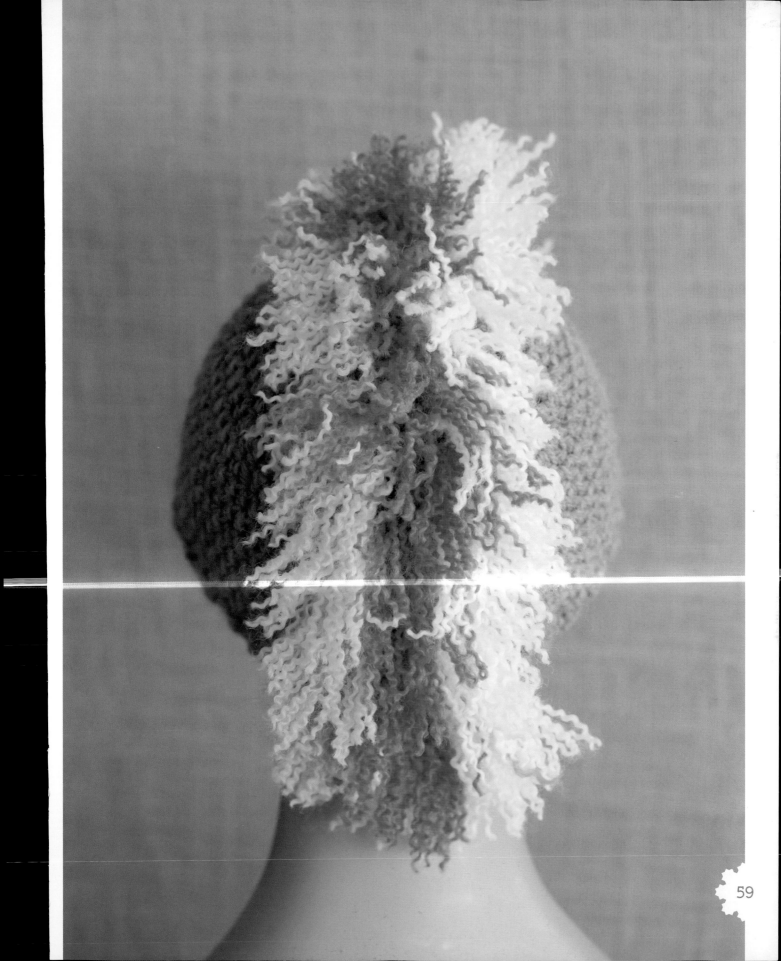

voodoo

Skulls aren't just for Halloween anymore! Allow the boy in your life to channel his inner skeleton year round with this fun design. The facial features are appliquéd on separately, making this hat a breeze to construct.

Yarn

Spud and Chloe Sweater (55% mercerized wool, 45% organic cotton; 160 yds/146m per 3.5oz/100g ball) or similar medium weight yarn in colors:

- no. 7517 Igloo (MC), 1 (2, 2) skeins
- no. 7522 Penguin (CC), 1 skein

Hooks and Notions

Size US J/10 (6mm) crochet hook or size needed to obtain gauge

Size US H/8 (5mm) (for eyes and nose, size S)

Size US I/9 (5.5mm) (for eyes and nose, size M)

Fabric stiffener (optional)

Yarn needle

Finished Measurements

Boys' S (Boys' M, Boys' L):

19" (48.3cm) (20" [50.8cm], 21" [53.3cm])

Gauge

First 8 rnds in pattern = 4¼" (11cm)

✳ SPECIAL STITCHES

Magic Loop technique: See Stitch Glossary for details.

✳ PATTERN NOTES

When working beg rnds, the circle will not be perfectly round.

Hat is worked using largest hook for all sizes. Smaller sized hooks are used for appliqués based on finished hat size.

CROCHET THE HAT

Rnd 1 (RS): Starting with MC, J hook, and magic lp technique, ch 1; 6 sc in lp. Join with a sl st to first sc. (6 sc)

Rnd 2: Ch 1; *(sc, ch 1) in each sc around. Join with a sl st to first sc. Turn. (6 sc, 6 ch-1 sps)

Rnd 3: Sl st to first ch-1 sp, ch 1; (sc, ch 1) in same sp, {[sc, ch 1] 2 times in next ch-1 sp, (sc, ch 1) in next ch-1 sp} 2 times. [Sc, ch 1] 2 times in last ch-1 sp. Join with a sl st to first sc. (9 sc, 9 ch-1 sps)

Rnd 4: Sl st to first ch-1 sp, ch 1; (sc, ch 1) in same sp and next ch-1 sp, {[sc, ch 1] 2 times in next ch-1 sp, (sc, ch 1) in next 2 ch-1 sps} 2 times. [Sc, ch 1] 2 times in last ch-1 sp. Join with a sl st to first sc. (12 sc, 12 ch-1 sps)

Rnd 5: Sl st to first ch-1 sp, ch 1; (sc, ch 1) in same sp and next 2 ch-1 sps, {[sc, ch 1] 2 times in next ch-1 sp, (sc, ch 1) in next 3 ch-1 sps} 2 times. [Sc, ch 1] 2 times in last ch-1 sp. Join with a sl st to first sc. (15 sc, 15 ch-1 sps)

Rnd 6: Sl st to first ch-1 sp, ch 1; (sc, ch 1) in same sp and next 3 ch-1 sps, {[sc, ch 1] 2 times in next ch-1 sp, (sc, ch 1) in next 4 ch-1 sps} 2 times. [Sc, ch 1] 2 times in last ch-1 sp. Join with a sl st to first sc. (18 sc, 18 ch-1 sps)

Rnd 7: Sl st to first ch-1 sp, ch 1; (sc, ch 1) in same sp and next 4 ch-1 sps, {[sc, ch 1] 2 times in next ch-1 sp, (sc, ch 1) in next 5 ch-1 sps} 2 times. [Sc, ch 1] 2 times in last ch-1 sp. Join with a sl st to first sc. (21 sc, 21 ch-1 sps)

Rnd 8: Sl st to first ch-1 sp, ch 1; (sc, ch 1) in same sp and next 5 ch-1 sps, {[sc, ch 1] 2 times in next ch-1 sp, (sc, ch 1) in next 6 ch-1 sps} 2 times. [Sc, ch 1] 2 times in last ch-1 sp. Join with a sl st to first sc. (24 sc, 24 ch-1 sps)

Rnd 9: Sl st to first ch-1 sp, ch 1; (sc, ch 1) in same sp and next 6 ch-1 sps, {[sc, ch 1] 2 times in next ch-1 sp, (sc, ch 1) in next 7 ch-1 sps} 2 times. [Sc, ch 1] 2 times in last ch-1 sp. Join with a sl st to first sc. (27 sc, 27 ch-1 sps)

Rnd 10: Sl st to first ch-1 sp, ch 1; (sc, ch 1) in same sp and next 7 ch-1 sps, {[sc, ch 1] 2 times in next ch-1 sp, (sc, ch 1) in next 8 ch-1 sps} 2 times. [Sc, ch 1] 2 times in last ch-1 sp. Join with a sl st to first sc. (30 sc, 30 ch-1 sps)

Rnd 11: Sl st to first ch-1 sp, ch 1; (sc, ch 1) in same sp and next 8 ch-1 sps, {[sc, ch 1] 2 times in next ch-1 sp, (sc, ch 1) in next 9 ch-1 sps} 2 times. [Sc, ch 1] 2 times in last ch-1 sp. Join with a sl st to first sc. (33 sc, 33 ch-1 sps)

SIZE M AND L

Rnd 12: Sl st to first ch-1 sp, ch 1; (sc, ch 1) in same sp and next 9 ch-1 sps, {[sc, ch 1] 2 times in next ch-1 sp, (sc, ch 1) in next 10 ch-1 sps} 2 times. [Sc, ch 1] 2 times in last ch-1 sp. Join with a sl st to first sc. (36 sc, 36 ch-1 sps)

SIZE L

Rnd 13: Ch 1; sl st to first ch-1 sp, ch 1; (sc, ch 1) in same sp and next 10 ch-1 sps, {[sc, ch 1] 2 times in next ch-1 sp, (sc, ch 1) in next 11 ch-1 sps} 2 times. [Sc, ch 1] 2 times in last ch-1 sp. Join with a sl st to first sc. (39 sc, 39 ch-1 sps)

ALL SIZES

Rnd 12 (13, 14): Sl st to first ch-1 sp, ch 3 (counts as first dc); dc in same ch sp. 2 dc in each ch-1 sp around. Join with a sl st to 3rd ch of beg ch-3. (66 [72, 78] dc)

Rnd 13 (14, 15): Sl st in next dc, sl st into sp bet dc just used and next dc. Ch 1; (sc, ch 1) in same area, *sk next 2 dc, (sc, ch 1) in sp bet last dc sk and next dc. Rep from * around. Join with a sl st to first sc.

Rnds 14–15 (15–16, 16–17): Sl st to first ch-1 sp. Ch 1; (sc, ch 1) in each ch-1 sp around. Join with a sl st to first sc.

Rnds 16–23 (17–24, 18–29): Rep Rnds 12–15 (13–16, 14–17) 2 (2, 3) times.

SIZE M ONLY
Rnds 25-26: Rep Rnds 15–16.

First Earflap

Row 1: Sl st to first ch-1 sp, ch 1; (sc, ch 1) in same sp, [(sc, ch 1) in next ch-1 sp] 6 (7, 9) times. Sc in next ch-1 sp. Turn. (8 [9, 11] sc and 7 [8, 10] ch-1 sps)

Row 2: Sl st to first ch-1 sp, ch 1; (sc, ch 1) in same sp, [(sc, ch 1) in next ch-1 sp] 5 (6, 8) times. Sc in next ch-1 sp. Turn. (7 [8, 10] sc and 6 [7, 9] ch-1 sps)

Row 3: Sl st to first ch-1 sp, ch 1; (sc, ch 1) in same sp, [(sc, ch 1) in next ch-1 sp] 4 (5, 7) times. Sc in next ch-1 sp. Turn. (6 [7, 9] sc and 5 [6, 8] ch-1 sps)

Row 4: Sl st to first ch-1 sp, ch 1; (sc, ch 1) in same sp, [(sc, ch 1) in next ch-1 sp] 3 (4, 6) times. Sc in next ch-1 sp. Turn. (5 [6, 8] sc and 4 [5, 7] ch-1 sps)

Row 5: Sl st to first ch-1 sp, ch 1; (sc, ch 1) in same sp, [(sc, ch 1) in next ch-1 sp] 2 (3, 5) times. Sc in next ch-1 sp. Turn. (4 [5, 7] sc and 3 [4, 6] ch-1 sps)

SIZE S
Row 6: Sl st to first ch-1 sp, ch 1; (sc, ch 2) in same sp, sc in last ch-1 sp. Fasten off. (2 sc and 1 ch-2 sp)

SIZE M
Row 6: Sl st to first ch-1 sp, ch 1; (sc, ch 1) in same sp, [(sc, ch 1) in next ch-1 sp] 2 times. Sc in next ch-1 sp. Turn. (4 sc and 3 ch-1 sps)

Row 7: Sl st to first ch-1 sp, ch 1; (sc, ch 2) in same sp, sc in last ch-1 sp. Fasten off. (2 sc and 1 ch-2 sp)

SIZE L
Row 6: Sl st to first ch-1 sp, ch 1; (sc, ch 1) in same sp, [(sc, ch 1) in next ch-1 sp] 4 times. Sc in next ch-1 sp. Turn. (6 sc and 5 ch-1 sps)

Row 7: Sl st to first ch-1 sp, ch 1; (sc, ch 1) in same sp, [(sc, ch 1) in next ch-1 sp] 3 times. Sc in next ch-1 sp. Turn. (5 sc and 4 ch-1 sps)

Row 8: Sl st to first ch-1 sp, ch 1; (sc, ch 1) in same sp, [(sc, ch 1) in next ch-1 sp] 2 times. Sc in next ch-1 sp. Turn. (4 sc and 3 ch-1 sps)

Row 9: Sl st to first ch-1 sp, ch 1; (sc, ch 2) in same sp, sc in last ch-1 sp. Fasten off. (2 sc and 1 ch-2 sp)

Second Earflap

Row 1: Sk next 4 (5, 6) ch-1 sps on last row of hat. Join MC with a sl st to next ch-1 sp, ch 1; (sc, ch 1) in same sp, [(sc, ch 1) in next ch-1 sp] 6 (7, 9) times. Sc in next ch-1 sp. Turn. (8 [9, 11] sc and 7 [8, 10] ch-1 sps)

Rep Rows 2–6 (2–7, 2–9) of first earflap.

Eyes (make 2)

Row 1: With CC and H (I, J) hook, ch 10, sc in 2nd ch from the hook and each ch across. Turn. (9 sc)

Row 2: Ch 1; 2 sc in first sc, sc in next 6 sc, sc dec over the last 2 sc. Turn. (9 sc)

Row 3: Ch 1; sc dec over first 2 sc, sc in next 6 sc, 2 sc in last sc. Turn.

Rows 4–5: Rep Rows 2 and 3. Complete trim for first and second eye.

First Eye Trim

Turn work 90° and place 5 sc along edge of rows. Turn 90° and working in unused lps of beg ch, sc in next 8 sts, 2 sc in next st. Turn work 90° and place 5 sc along edge. Turn work 90° and working into Row 5, 2 sc in first st, sc in next 8 sts. Join with a sl st to first sc in trim. Finish off leaving a long tail for sewing. (30 sc)

Second Eye Trim

Ch 1, turn. 2 sc in first st, sc in next 8 sts. Turn 90° and place 5 sc along row edge. Turn 90° and working in unused lps of beg ch, 2 sc in first st, sc in next 8 sts. Turn 90° and place 5 sc along row edge. Join with a sl st to first sc. Finish off leaving a long tail for sewing. (30 sc)

Nose

With CC, H (I, J) hook, and working with a magic lp, (ch 3, tr, ch 1, sc, ch 1, tr, ch 3, sl st) in magic lp. Pull to tighten. Finish off leaving a long tail for sewing.

Finishing

Sew eyes and nose onto hat using long tails. Using CC, embroider mouth design similar to picture. Cut twelve 22" (56cm) (24", 26" [61cm, 66cm]) lengths of each color yarn. Use 6 strands of each color per side. Fold strands in half and insert into ch-2 sp at bottom of earflap. Fold over and pull long end through lp to secure. Separate strands into 3 sections mixing the colors. Braid. Tie ends in an overhand knot and trim. Rep for second side.

canyon stripes set

SKILL LEVEL: EASY

This set is a classic. Different stripes of varying widths and lots of color accents create a simple crochet style. The hat can be folded at the brim or worn slouchy. The fringed scarf makes a great finishing touch.

Yarn

Lion Brand Yarns Heartland (100% acrylic; 251 yds/230m per 5 oz/142g ball) or similar medium weight yarn in colors:

no. 153 Black Canyon (MC), 1 skein

no. 158 Yellowstone (CC1), 1 skein

no. 105 Glacier Bay (CC2), 1 skein

no. 098 Acadia (CC3), 1 skein

no. 173 Everglades (CC4), 1 skein

Hooks and Notions

Size US J/10 (6mm) crochet hook or size needed to obtain gauge

Yarn needle

Finished Measurements

Hat: Boys' S (Boys' M, Boys' L):

19" (48.3cm) (20" [50.8cm], 21" [53.3cm])

Scarf: one size

5½" × 40" (14cm × 101.6cm)

Gauge

Hat: first 8 rnds in pattern = 3¾" (9.5cm)

Scarf: 13 sts and 9 rows in hdc = 4" (10.2cm)

✳ SPECIAL STITCHES

Magic Loop technique: See Stitch Glossary for details.

✳ PATTERN NOTES

Ch 1 at beg of each hdc row is worked loosely to the height of a hdc and does not count as a st.

Ch 2 at beg of each dc row is worked loosely to the height of a dc and does not count as a st.

CROCHET THE HAT

Rnd 1: Starting with MC and magic lp technique, ch 1; 8 hdc in lp. Join with a sl st to first hdc. (8 hdc)

Rnd 2: Ch 1; 2 hdc in each st around. Join with a sl st to first hdc. (16 hdc)

Rnd 3: Ch 1; *hdc in first st, 2 hdc in next st. Rep from * around. Join with a sl st to first hdc. (24 hdc)

Rnd 4: Ch 1; *hdc in first 2 sts, 2 hdc in next st. Rep from * around. Join with a sl st to first hdc. (32 hdc)

Rnd 5: Ch 1; *hdc in first 3 sts, 2 hdc in next st. Rep from * around. Join with a sl st to first hdc. (40 hdc)

Rnd 6: Ch 1; *hdc in first 4 sts, 2 hdc in next st. Rep from * around. Join with a sl st to first hdc. (48 hdc)

SIZE M AND L
Rnd 7: Ch 1; *hdc in first 5 sts, 2 hdc in next st. Rep from * around. Join with a sl st to first hdc. (56 hdc)

SIZE L
Rnd 8: Ch 1; *hdc in first 6 sts, 2 hdc in next st. Rep from * around. Join with a sl st to first hdc. (64 hdc)

ALL SIZES
Rnd 7 (8, 9): Ch 1; hdc in each st around. Join with a sl st and CC1 to first hdc. (48 [56, 64] hdc)

Rnd 8 (9, 10): Working in BL, ch 1; sc in each st around. Join with a sl st and MC to first sc.

Rnd 9 (10, 11): Working in BL, ch 1; hdc in each st around. Join with a sl st and CC2 to first hdc.

Rnd 10 (11, 12): Working in BL, ch 1; hdc in each st around. Join with a sl st and MC to first hdc.

Rnd 11 (12, 13): Working in BL, ch 1; hdc in each st around. Join with a sl st and CC3 to first hdc.

Rnd 12 (13, 14): Working in BL, ch 2; dc in each st around. Join with a sl st and MC to first dc.

Rnd 13 (14, 15): Working in BL, ch 1; hdc in each st around. Join with a sl st and CC4 to first hdc.

Rnd 14 (15, 16): Working in BL, ch 1; hdc in each st around. Join with a sl st to first hdc.

Rnd 15 (16, 17): Working in both lps, ch 1; hdc in each hdc around. Join with a sl st and MC to first hdc.

Rnd 16 (17, 18): Working in BL, ch 1; hdc in each st around. Join with a sl st to first hdc.

Rnds 17–23 (18–24, 19–25): Working in both lps, ch 1; hdc in each hdc around. Join with a sl st to first hdc.

Rnd 24 (25, 26): Ch 1; sc in each st around. Join with a sl st to first sc. Finish off.

Finishing

Weave in ends.

Row 1: Starting with MC, ch 19; hdc in second ch from hook and each ch across. Turn. (18 hdc)

Rows 2–8: Ch 1; hdc in each st across. Change to CC1 at end of Row 8. Turn.

Row 9: Ch 1; sc in each st across. Change to MC. Turn.

Row 10: Ch 1; hdc in each st across. Change to CC2. Turn.

Row 11: Rep Row 10. Change to MC. Turn.

Row 12: Rep Row 10. Change to CC3. Turn.

Row 13: Ch 2, dc in each st across. Change to MC. Turn.

Row 14: Rep Row 10. Change to CC4. Turn.

Rows 15–16: Rep Row 10. Change to MC. Turn.

Row 17: Rep Row 10. Change to CC3. Turn.

Row 18: Rep Row 13.

Row 19: Rep Row 10. Change to CC2. Turn.

Row 20: Rep Row 10. Change to MC. Turn.

Row 21: Rep Row 10. Change to CC1. Turn.

Row 22: Rep Row 9.

Rows 23–38: Rep Row 2. Change to CC1 at end of Row 38.

Rows 39–68: Rep Rows 9-38.

Rows 69–90: Rep Rows 9-30. Finish off.

Weave in ends. Using all CC yarns, cut into lengths of 8" (20.3cm) and attach via fringe method to scarf ends as desired.

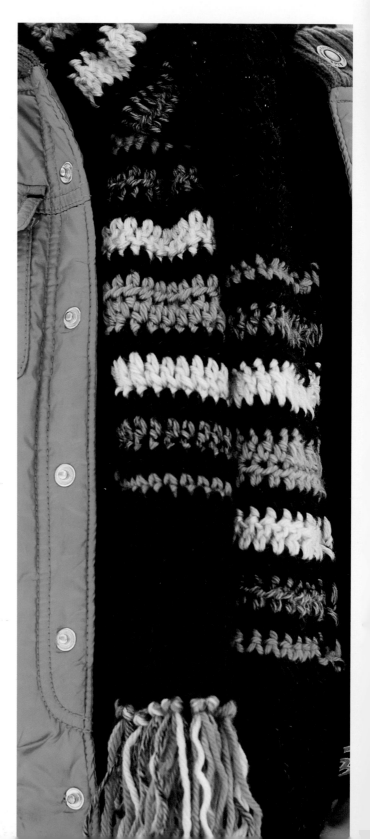

CHAPTER THREE

women's hats

The designs in this chapter are geared towards women who like to have fun outdoors, but who aren't willing to sacrifice style for function. These stylish patterns range in difficulty, so whether you're a novice or looking for a challenge, there's a design here to satisfy you.

blue diamond

A great all-weather hat, this bucket style can easily keep the sun out of your eyes, keep your head from becoming sunburnt, and keep you warm. The fun cabled design provides a slight crocheting challenge while adding a bit of intricacy to the finished hat.

Yarn

Berroco Vintage DK (52% acrylic, 40% wool, 8% nylon; 288 yds/263m per 3.5 oz/100g ball) or similar light weight yarn in color no. 2149 Forget-Me-Not, 1 skein

Hooks and Notions

Size US H/8 (5mm) crochet hook or size needed to obtain gauge

Stitch marker

Yarn needle

For optional pearl accents:

Sewing and/or beading thread

13-4mm Round Glass Pearls – color Ecru

Beading needle

Finished Measurements

Women's S (Women's M, Women's L)

21" (53.3cm) (22" [55.9cm], 23" [58.4cm])

Gauge

First 9 rnds in pattern = 4" (10.2cm)

✳ SPECIAL STITCHES

Magic Loop technique: See Stitch Glossary for details.

✳ PATTERN NOTES

First st of each rnd is worked in same st as joining.

Ch 1 at beg of rnd does not count as a st unless stated otherwise.

CROCHET THE HAT

Rnd 1: With magic lp technique, ch 1; 8 hdc in ring. Join with a sl st to first hdc. (8 hdc)

Rnd 2: Ch 1; 2 hdc in each st around. Join with a sl st to first hdc. (16 hdc)

Rnd 3: Ch 1; *hdc in next st, 2 hdc in next st. Rep from * around. Join with a sl st to first hdc. (24 hdc)

Rnd 4: Ch 1; *hdc in next 2 sts, 2 hdc in next st. Rep from * around. Join with a sl st to first hdc. (32 hdc)

Rnd 5: Ch 1; *hdc in next 3 sts, 2 hdc in next st. Rep from * around. Join with a sl st to first hdc. (40 hdc)

Rnd 6: Ch 1; *hdc in next 4 sts, 2 hdc in next st. Rep from * around. Join with a sl st to first hdc. For size S, place st marker on fourth st in rnd. (48 hdc)

Rnd 7: Ch 1; *hdc in next 5 sts, 2 hdc in next st. Rep from * around. Join with a sl st to first hdc. For size M, place st marker on fifth st in rnd. (56 hdc)

Rnd 8: Ch 1; *hdc in next 6 sts, 2 hdc in next st. Rep from * around. Join with a sl st to first hdc. For size L, place st marker on sixth st in rnd. (64 hdc)

SIZE S
Rnd 9: Ch 1; sc in next 5 sts. Sk next st, fptr in marked st 3 rows below. [Sc in next 3 sts, fptr in same st 2 rows below leaving last 2 lps on hook, sk 2 sts on same row as last fptr, fptr on next st and finishing through all 3 lps on hook, sk next st on this round] 2 times. Sc in each rem st around. Join with a sl st to first sc.

SIZE M
Rnd 9: Ch 1; *hdc in next 7 sts, 2 hdc in next st. Rep from * around. Join with a sl st to first hdc. (72 hdc)

Rnd 10: Ch 1; sc in next 5 sts. Sk next st, fptr in marked st 3 rows below. [Sc in next 3 sts, fptr in same st 2 rows below leaving last 2 lps on hook, sk 2 sts on same row as last fptr, fptr on next st and finishing through all 3 lps on hook, sk next st on this round] 2 times. Sc in each rem st around. Join with a sl st to first sc.

SIZE L
Rnd 9: Ch 1; *hdc in next 7 sts, 2 hdc in next st. Rep from * around. Join with a sl st to first hdc. (72 hdc)

Rnd 10: Ch 1; *hdc in next 8 sts, 2 hdc in next st. Rep from * around. Join with a sl st to first hdc. (80 hdc)

Rnd 11: Ch 1; sc in next 5 sts. Sk next st, fptr in marked st 3 rows below. [Sc in next 3 sts, fptr in same st 2 rows below leaving last 2 lps on hook, sk 2 sts on same row as last fptr, fptr on next st and finishing through all 3 lps on hook, sk next st on this rnd] 2 times. Sc in each rem st around. Join with a sl st to first sc.

ALL SIZES
Rnds 10–11 (11–12, 12–13): Ch 1; hdc in each st around. Join with a sl st to first hdc.

Rnd 12 (13, 14): Ch 1; sc in next 9 sts. Fptr around first fptr of rnd 3 rows below leaving last 2 lps on hook, fptr around third fptr of same rnd and finish through all 3 lps on hook. Sk next st in this rnd, sc in next 3 sts. Fptr around second fptr of same previous rnd leaving last 2 lps on hook, fptr around fifth fptr of same previous rnd and finishing through all 3 lps on hook. Sk next st in this rnd, sc in next 3 sts. Fptr around fourth fptr of same previous rnd leaving last 2 lps on hook, fptr around sixth fptr of same previous rnd and finishing through all 3 lps on hook. Sc in each st around. Join with a sl st to first sc.

Rnds 13–14 (14–15, 15–16): Ch 1; hdc in each st around. Join with a sl st to first hdc.

FIGURE 1

FIGURE 2

FIGURE 3

Rnd 15 (16, 17): Ch 1; sc in next 9 sts. Sk next st, fptr in second fptr 3 rnds below (Figure 1). Sc in next 3 sts, fptr in first fptr 3 rnds below leaving last 2 lps on hook (Figure 2), fptr on fourth fptr on same rnd and finishing through all 3 lps on hook (Figure 3), sk next st on this rnd. Sc in next 3 sts, fptr in third fptr 3 rnds below leaving last 2 lps on hook, fptr on sixth fptr on same rnd and finishing through all 3 lps on hook, sk next st on this round. Sc in next 3 sts, fptr on fifth fptr 3 rnds below. Sk next st, sc in each rem st around. Join with a sl st to first sc.

Rnds 16–17 (17–18, 18–19): Ch 1; hdc in each st around. Join with a sl st to first hdc.

Rnd 18 (19, 20): Ch 1; sc in next 13 sts. fptr around first fptr of rnd 3 rnds below leaving last 2 lps on hook, fptr around third fptr of same rnd and finishing through all 3 lps on hook. Sk next st in this rnd, sc in next 3 sts. Fptr around second fptr of same previous rnd leaving last 2 lps on hook, fptr around fifth fptr of same previous rnd and finishing through all 3 lps on hook. Sk next st in this rnd, sc in next 3 sts. Fptr around fourth fptr of same previous rnd leaving last 2 lps on hook, fptr around sixth fptr of same previous rnd and finishing through all 3 lps on hook. Sc in each st around. Join with a sl st to first sc.

Rnds 19–20 (20–21, 21–22): Ch 1; hdc in each st around. Join with a sl st to first hdc.

Rnd 21 (22, 23): Ch 1; sc in next 13 sts. Sk next st, fptr in second fptr 3 rnds below. Sc in next 3 sts, fptr in first fptr 3 rnds below leaving last 2 lps on hook, fptr on fourth fptr on same rnd and finishing through all 3 lps on hook, sk next st on this rnd. Sc in next 3 sts, fptr in third fptr 3 rnds below leaving last 2 lps on hook, fptr on sixth fptr on same rnd and finishing through all 3 lps on hook, sk next st on this rnd. Sc in next 3 sts, fptr on fifth fptr 3 rnds below. Sk next st, sc in each rem st around. Join with a sl st to first sc.

Rnds 22–23 (23–24, 24–25): Ch1; hdc in each st around. Join with a sl st to first hdc.

Rnd 24 (25, 26): Ch 1; sc in next 17 sts. Fptr around first fptr of rnd 3 rnds below leaving last 2 lps on hook, fptr around third fptr of same rnd and finishing through all 3 lps on hook. Sk next st in this rnd, sc in next 3 sts. Fptr around second fptr of same previous rnd leaving last 2 lps on hook, fptr around fifth fptr of same previous rnd and finishing through all 3 lps on hook. Sk next st in this rnd, sc in next 3 sts. Fptr around fourth fptr of same previous rnd leaving last 2 lps on hook, fptr around sixth fptr of same previous rnd and finishing through all 3 lps on hook. Sc in each st around. Join with a sl st to first sc.

Rnd 25 (26, 27): Ch1; hdc in each st around. Join with a sl st to first hdc. (64 [72, 80] hdc)

Rnd 26 (27, 28): Ch 1; *hdc in next 3 sts, 2 hdc in next st. Rep from * around. Join with a sl st to first hdc. (80 [90, 100] hdc)

Rnd 27 (28, 29): Ch 1; hdc in each st around. Join with a sl st to first hdc.

Rnd 28 (29, 30): Ch 1; rev sc in each st around. Join with a sl st to first rev sc. Finish off.

Finishing

Weave in ends. Sew optional pearls into center of each cable diamond (Figure 4).

FIGURE 4

aspen

Imagine a leisurely walk: tiny snowflakes are falling as the sun sets. Your ears are probably the coldest parts of your body, so keep them warm with this fun earflap hat that features a snowflake design, large pom-poms and a fun and funky color combination. This hat will work up quickly, just in time for that walk this weekend.

Yarn

Red Heart Soft Baby Steps (100% acrylic; 256 yds/234m per 5 oz/142g ball) or similar medium weight yarn in colors:

no. 9630 Lime (MC), 1 skein

no. 9536 Light Grape (CC), 1 skein

Hooks and Notions

Size US I/9 (5.5mm) crochet hook or size needed to obtain gauge

Yarn needle

Finished Measurements

Women's S/M (Women's M/L):

21"–22" (53.3cm–55.9cm) (22"–23" [55.9cm–58.4cm])

Gauge

First 6 rnds in pattern = 4" (10.2cm)

✳ SPECIAL STITCHES

Magic Loop technique: See Stitch Glossary for details.

✳ PATTERN NOTES

Fist st of each rnd is worked in same st as joining.

Ch 2 at beg of rnd does not count as a st unless stated otherwise.

CROCHET THE HAT

Rnd 1: With MC and magic lp technique, ch 2; 12 dc in ring. Join with a sl st to first dc. (12 dc)

Rnd 2: Ch 2; 2 dc in each st around. Join with a sl st to first dc. (24 dc)

Rnd 3: Ch 2; *dc in first st, 2 dc in next st. Rep from * around. Join with a sl st to first dc. (36 dc)

Rnd 4: Ch 2; *dc in first 2 sts, 2 dc in next st. Rep from * around. Join with a sl st to first dc. (48 dc)

Rnd 5: Ch 2; *dc in first 3 sts, 2 dc in next st. Rep from * around. Join with a sl st to first dc. (60 dc)

SIZE M/L
Rnd 6: Ch 2; *dc in first 4 sts, 2 dc in next st. Rep from * around. Join with a sl st to first dc. (72 dc)

ALL SIZES
Rnd 6 (7): Ch 2; dc in each dc around. Join with a sl st and CC to first dc. (60 [72] dc)

Rnd 7 (8): Ch 5 (counts as first dc and ch-2 sp); dc dec over next st and fourth st. Sk 3 sts in bet. Ch 2, dc in next st. *Ch 2, dc dec over next st and fourth st, ch 2, dc in next st. Rep from * around. Join with a sl st to third ch of beg ch-5.

Rnd 8 (9): Ch 3 (counts as first dc); *(dc, ch 3, dc) in dec st of previous row, dc in next dc. Rep from * around. Join with a sl st and MC to third ch of beg ch-3.

Rnd 9 (10): Ch 2; dc in each st and ch around. Join with a sl st and CC to first dc.

Rnds 10–12 (11–13): Rep rnds 7–9 (8–10). Fasten off at end of Rnd 12 (13). (60 [72] dc)

First Earflap

Row 1: Attach CC with a sl st to next st on Rnd 12 (13). Ch 5 (counts as first dc and ch-2 sp); [dc dec over next st and fourth st. Sk 3 sts in bet. Ch 2, dc in next st, ch 2] 3 times. Dc in next st. Turn.

Row 2: Ch 3 (counts as first dc); [(dc, ch 3, dc) in dec st of previous row, dc in next dc] 2 times. (Dc, ch 3, dc) in dec st of previous row, dc in third ch of beg ch-5. Change to MC, turn.

Row 3: Ch 3 (counts as first dc), dc in next st. [2 dc in next ch-3 sp, dc3tog over next 3 sts] 2 times. 2 dc in next ch-3 sp, dc in last 2 sts. Turn. (12 dc)

Row 4: Ch 3 (counts as first dc); dc in next st, dc3tog over next 3 sts, dc in next 2 sts, dc3tog over next 3 sts, dc in next st, dc in turning ch. Fasten off. (8 dc)

Second Earflap

Row 1: Sk next 17 (27) sts on Rnd 12 (13), attach CC with a sl st to next st on rnd. Ch 5 (counts as first dc and ch-2 sp); [dc dec over next st and fourth st. Sk 3 sts in bet. Ch 2, dc in next st, ch 2] 3 times. Dc in next st. Turn.

Rep Rows 2–4 of first earflap. Do not fasten off at the end of Row 4. Continue on to trim.

Trim

Ch 1; turn. Sc in first st, ch 4, sk 6 sts, sc in last st. Evenly sp 7 sc along earflap edge, sc in each st across back of hat. Evenly sp 7 sc along side of next earflap, sc in next st, ch 4, sk 6 sts, sc in last st of earflap Row 4. Evenly sp 7 sc along earflap edge, sc in each st across front of hat. Evenly sp 7 sc along side of first earflap. Join with a sl st to first st in trim. Finish off.

Finishing

Weave in ends. Make 2 large pom-poms using both colors of yarn held together. Attach to last row of earflaps. Sample pom-poms measure 5½" (14cm), but you can make yours whatever size you want.

serendipity

S louchy hats are the ultimate accessory: they add a touch of style all while hiding a bad hair day. This pattern will challenge you with construction techniques, but it is worth the time and effort involved. I'm positive you will love the outcome.

Yarn

Bernat Cotton-ish (55% cotton, 45% acrylic; 282 yds/258m per 2.4 oz/70g ball) or similar light weight yarn in colors:

>   no. 85700 Jade Jersey (MC), 1 skein
>
>   no. 85044 Grey T-shirt (CC1), 1 skein
>
>   no. 85628 Cotton Harvest (CC2), 1 skein

Hooks and Notions

Size US G/6 (4mm) crochet hook or size needed to obtain gauge

Yarn needle

Finished Measurements

Women's S (Women's M, Women's L):

21" (53.3cm) (22" [55.9cm], 23" [58.4cm])

Gauge

14 rows and 19 sts in pattern = 4" (10.2cm)

✳ PATTERN NOTES

Hat is worked in the rnd to form a tube. Hat band is worked onto the tube at one end and then the opposite end is gathered closed.

Body of hat is essentially the same for all sizes. Band is worked to fit size.

Band is worked in rows vertically to the hat.

CROCHET THE HAT

Rnd 1: With MC and leaving a long tail, ch 100; sc in second ch from hook and each ch across. Being careful not to twist work, join with a sl st to first sc to form a lp. (99 sc)

Rnd 2: Ch 3 (counts as first dc); (4 dc, ch 1) in same st as joining. *[Sk next st, (dc, ch 1) in next st] 3 times. Sk next st, (dc5tog, ch 1) over next 5 sts, [sk next st, (dc, ch 1) in next st] 3 times. Sk next st, ** (5dc, ch 1) in next st. Rep from * around until 19 sts rem. Rep from * to ** one more time. Join with a sl st to third ch of beg ch-3.

Rnd 3: Ch 1; sc in same st as joining and each st and ch-1 sp around. Join with CC1 and a sl st to first sc.

Rnd 4: Ch 1; working in BL, sc in same st as joining and each st around. Join with CC2 and a sl st to first sc.

Rnd 5: Ch 1; working in BL, sc in same st as joining and each st around. Join with a sl st to first sc.

Rnd 6: Sl st in first 3 sts, rep Rnd 2.

Rnd 7: Rep Rnd 3.

Rnd 8: Rep Rnd 4 with CC1, changing to MC at the end of rnd.

Rnds 9–10: Rep Rnds 5–6.

Rnd 11: Rep Rnd 3.

Rnd 12: Rep Rnd 4 with CC1, changing to CC2 at the end of rnd.

Rnds 13–32: Rep Rnds 5–12.

Rnds 33–35: Rep Rnds 5–7.

Rnd 36: Ch 1; sc in same st as joining, *sl st in next 3 sts, sc in next 3 sts, hdc in next 3 sts, dc5tog over next 5 sts, hdc in next 3 sts, sc in next 3 sts. Rep from * around until 19 sts rem. Sl st in next 3 sts, sc in next 3 sts, hdc in next 3 sts, dc5tog over next 5 sts, hdc in next 3 sts, sc in last 2 sts. Join with a sl st to first sc.

Rnd 37: Ch 1; sc in same st as joining and each st around. Join with a sl st to first sc. (80 sc)

SIZE S
Rnd 38: Ch 1; sc in same st as joining and next 5 sts, sc dec over next 2 sts. *Sc in next 6 sts, sc dec over next 2 sts. Rep from * around and join with a sl st to first sc. (70 sc)

SIZE M
Rnd 38: Ch 1; sc in same st as joining and next 13 sts, sc dec over next 2 sts. *Sc in next 14 sts, sc dec over next 2 sts. Rep from * around and join with a sl st to first sc. (75 sc)

SIZE L
Rnd 38: Ch 1; sc in same st as joining and each st around. Join with a sl st to first sc. (80 sc)

Band

Row 1: Ch 9; sl st in second ch from hook and each ch across. Sl st to next sc on hat Rnd 38 (Figure 1). Turn. (8 sl st)

Row 2: Ch 1; working in BL, sl st in each st across. Turn.

Row 3: Ch 1; working in BL, sl st in each st across. Sl st to next sc on hat Rnd 38. Turn.

Rows 4–70 (4-75, 4-80): Rep Rows 2–3. Sl st last row of band to first row of band. Finish off.

FIGURE 1
Work hat band in rows vertically to the hat.

Finishing

Weave in ends. With the long tail of the hat body beg ch, weave through Rnd 1 of hat and pull tightly to close.

city slicker set

Turbans are having their moment, and it's no secret why. They can easily be dressed up or dressed down to suit your desired look. Choose a deep, rich color and pair it with the versatile cowl, which can be worn long or wrapped around your neck to keep you warm. The stitch techniques used are very simple, but be sure to pay close attention to the unusual construction of the hat.

Yarn

Bernat Softee Chunky (100% acrylic; 108 yds/99m per 3.5 oz/100g ball) or similar super bulky weight yarn in color no. 28532 Wine, 3 skeins

Hooks and Notions

Size US L/11 (8mm) crochet hook or size needed to obtain gauge

Yarn needle

Finished Measurements

Hat: Women's S (Women's M, Women's L):

21" (53.3cm) (22" [55.9cm], 23" [58.4cm])

Cowl: one size

45" × 5" (114.3cm × 12.7cm)

Gauge

8 sts and 9 rows in sc = 4" (10.2cm)

✳ PATTERN NOTES

All sts are worked in the back loops (BL).

Hat is worked flat from brim to crown, folded and then sewn together. Band is crocheted separately and attached.

CROCHET THE HAT

Row 1: Leaving a long tail for seaming, Fsc 40 (42, 44). Turn. (40 [42, 44] sc)

Row 2 (RS): Ch 1; working in BL, sl st in first 2 sts, sc in each st across until 2 sts rem, sl st in last 2 sts. Turn.

Row 3–11 (3–12, 3–13): Rep Row 2.

Row 12 (13, 14): Ch 1; working in BL, sl st in first 4 sts, sc in each st across until 4 sts rem, sl st in last 4 sts. Turn.

Row 13 (14, 15): Ch 1; working in BL, sl st in first 6 sts, sc in each st across until 6 sts rem, sl st in last 6 sts. Turn.

Row 14 (15, 16): Ch 1; working in BL, sl st in first 8 sts, sc in next 10 (11, 12) sts, sl st in next st, sl st dec over next 2 sts (place marker). Sl st in next st, sc in next 10 (11, 12) sts, sl st in next 2 sts. Leave rem sts unworked. Turn.

Row 15 (16, 17): Ch 1; working in BL, sl st in first 2 sts, sc in next 10 (11, 12) sts, sl st in next 3 sts and move marker. Sc in next 10 (11, 12) sts, sl st in next 2 sts. Leave rem sts unworked. Turn.

Row 16 (17, 18): Ch 1; working in BL, sl st in first 2 sts, sc in next 10 (11, 12) sts, sl st dec over next st and third st (sk 1 st) (move marker). Sc in next 10 (11, 12) sts, sl st in next 2 sts.

Row 17 (18, 19): Ch 1; working in BL, sl st in first 2 sts, sc in next 9 (10, 11) sts, sl st dec over next st and third st (sk 1 st) (move marker). Sc in next 9 (10, 11) sts, sl st in next 2 sts.

Row 18 (19, 20): Ch 1; working in BL, sl st in first 2 sts, sc in next 7 (8, 9) sts, sl st in next st, sl st dec over next st and third st (sk 1 st) (move marker), sl st in next st. Sc in next 7 (8, 9) sts, sl st in next 2 sts.

Row 19 (20, 21): Ch 1; working in BL, sl st in first 2 sts, sc in next 7 (8, 9) sts, sl st dec over next st and third st (sk 1 st) (move marker). Sc in next 7 (8, 9) sts, sl st in next 2 sts. Finish off leaving a long tail for seaming.

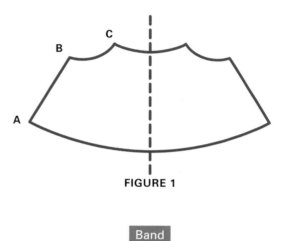

FIGURE 1

Band

Row 1: Ch 17 (18, 19); sl st in second ch from hook and each ch across. Turn. (16 [17, 18] sl sts)

Rows 2–10: Ch 1; working in BL, sl st in each st across. Turn. Finish off at end of Row 10 leaving a long tail for seaming.

Finishing

Fold in half at the marker (dotted line in figure 1) so that ribbing runs vertically. Using long tail, seam from fold to C. Using second long tail, seam from A to B being sure to match up ribbing. Weave end using a loose running st through A–B and pull tightly to gather. Wrap band around hat through opening and around gather just made. Seam band together on inside of hat. Tack to hat and seam opening closed if needed. Weave in ends.

CROCHET THE COWL

Row 1: Leaving a long tail for seaming, Fsc 80. Turn. (80 sc)

Row 2 (RS): Ch 1; working in BL, sl st in first 2 sts, sc in each st across until 2 sts rem, sl st in last 2 sts. Turn.

Rows 3–13: Rep Row 2. Finish off at end of Row 13 leaving a long tail for seaming.

Band

Row 1: Ch 19; sl st in second ch from hook and each ch across. Turn. (18 sl sts)

Rows 2–10: Ch 1; working in BL, sl st in each st across. Turn. Finish off at end of Row 10 leaving a long tail for seaming.

Finishing

Fold in half so that ribbing runs vertically. Using long tail, seam ends together to form a circle. Weave end using a loose running stitch through and pull tightly to gather. Wrap band around cowl and seam together on inside of cowl. Tack to cowl and tack in place if needed. Weave in ends.

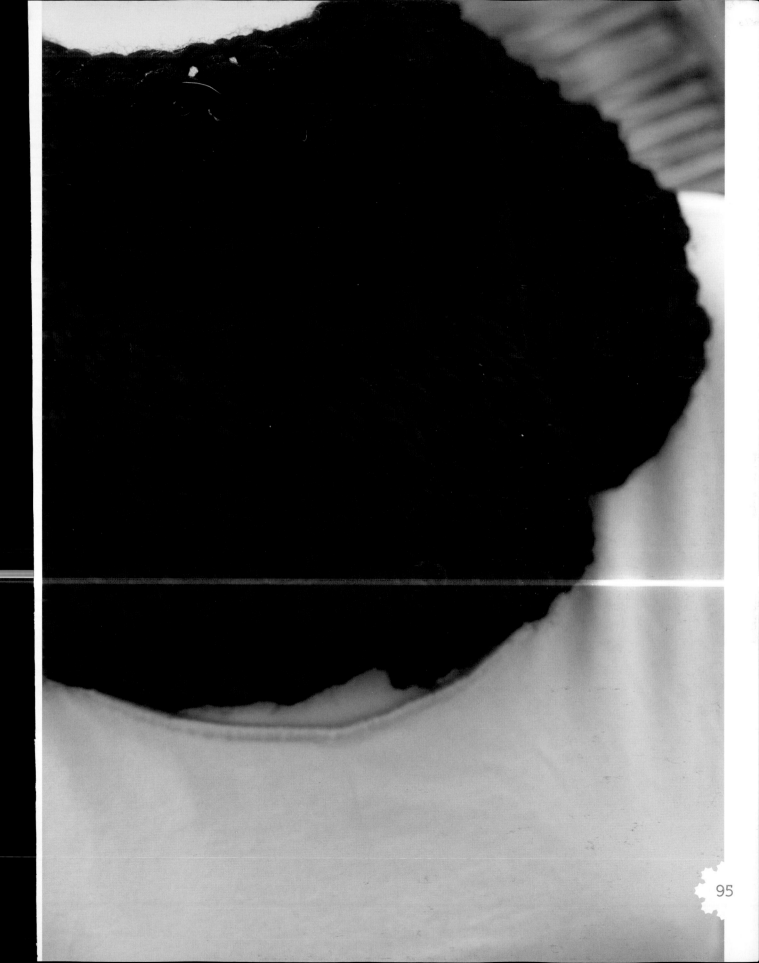

CHAPTER FOUR

men's hats

I can't tell you the number of men I see these days wearing some of the most unusual and creative hat designs. And yes, men crochet too! So gentlemen, why don't you grab a hook and create your very own one-of-a-kind hat? Or ladies, make one for that amazing man of yours to show him how much you care. Remember, hats make great gifts!

summit

This is such a fun and simple design. It works up quickly and looks amazing, perfect for a last-minute gift or a staple for any winter wardrobe.

Yarn

Plymouth Yarn Company Coffee Beenz (75% acrylic, 25% wool; 212 yds/193.9m per 3.5 oz/100g ball) or similar light weight yarn in color no. 9231 White Green-house, 1 skein

Hooks and Notions

Size US I/9 (5.5mm) crochet hook or size needed to obtain gauge

Size US H/8 (5mm) crochet hook

Yarn needle

Finished Measurements

Men's S (Men's M, Men's L)

22" (55.9cm) (23" [58.4cm], 24" [61cm])

Gauge

First 7 rnds in pattern, with larger hook = 4" (10.2cm)

✳ SPECIAL STITCHES

Magic Loop technique: See Stitch Glossary for details.

✳ PATTERN NOTES

Push tr to RS when finished with row.

First st in rnd is always worked in same st as joining.

CROCHET THE HAT

Rnd 1 (RS): Starting larger hook and magic lp technique, ch 1; 6 sc in lp. Join with a sl st to first sc. (6 sc)

Rnd 2: Ch 1; 2 sc in each st around. Join with a sl st to first sc. (12 sc)

Rnd 3: Ch 1; *sc in next st, (tr, sc) in next. Rep from * around. Join with a sl st to first sc. (12 sc and 6 tr)

Rnd 4: Ch 1; *sc in first 2 sts, 2 sc in next st. Rep from * around. Join with a sl st to first sc. (24 sc)

Rnd 5: Ch 1; *sc in first 3 sts, 2 sc in next st. Rep from * around. Join with a sl st to first sc. (30 sc)

Rnd 6: Ch 1; *sc in first 4 sts, (tr, sc) in next st. Rep from * around. Join with a sl st to first sc. (30 sc and 6 tr)

Rnd 7: Ch 1; *sc in first 5 sts, 2 sc in next st. Rep from * around. Join with a sl st to first sc. (42 sc)

Rnd 8: Ch1; sc in first 5 sts, [tr in next st, sc in next 6 sts] 5 times. Tr in next st, sc in last st. Join with a sl st to first sc. (36 sc and 6 tr)

Rnd 9: Ch 1; sc in first 2 sts, [(tr, sc) in next st, sc in next 7 sts] 5 times. (Tr, sc) in next st, sc in last 5 sts. Join with a sl st to first sc. (48 sc and 6 tr)

Rnd 10: Ch 1; *sc in first 8 sts, 2 sc in next st. Rep from * around. Join with a sl st to first sc. (60 sc)

Rnd 11: Ch 1; *sc in first 9 sts, 2 sc in next st. Rep from * around. Join with a sl st to first sc. (66 sc)

Rnd 12: Ch 1; sc in first st, ch 2, sk 2 sts, *sc in next st, ch 2

SIZE S
Rnd 13–14: Ch 1; sc in each st around. Join with a sl st to first sc. (72 sc)

SIZE M
Rnd 13: Ch 1; *sc in first 11 sts, 2 sc in next st. Rep from * around. Join with a sl st to first sc. (78 sc)

Rnd 14: Ch 1; sc in each st around. Join with a sl st to first sc. (78 sc)

SIZE L
Rnd 13: Ch 1; *sc in first 11 sts, 2 sc in next st. Rep from * around. Join with a sl st to first sc. (78 sc)

Rnd 14: Ch 1; *sc in first 12 sts, 2 sc in next st. Rep from * around. Join with a sl st to first sc. (84 sc)

ALL SIZES
Rnd 15: Ch 1; sc in first 4 sts, [tr in next st, sc in next 11 (12, 13) sts] 5 times. Tr in next st, sc in last 7 (8, 9) sts. Join with a sl st to first sc.

Rnds 16–17: Ch 1; sc in each st around. Join with a sl st to first sc.

Rnd 18: Ch 1; sc in first 10 sts, [tr in next st, sc in next 11 (12, 13) sts] 5 times. Tr in next 1 (2, 3) sts, sc in last st. Join with a sl st to first sc.

Rnds 19–20: Ch 1; sc in each st around. Join with a sl st to first sc.

Rnd 21: Ch 1; sc in first 3 sts, [tr in next st, sc in next 11 (12, 13) sts] 5 times. Tr in next st, sc in last 8 (9, 10) sts. Join with a sl st to first sc.

Rnds 22–23: Ch 1; sc in each st around. Join with a sl st to first sc.

Rnd 24: Ch 1; sc in first 8 sts, [tr in next st, sc in next 11 (12, 13) sts] 5 times. Tr in next st, sc in last 3 (4, 5) sts. Join with a sl st to first sc.

Rnds 25–26: Ch 1; sc in each st around. Join with a sl st to first sc.

Rnd 27: Rep Rnd 15.

Rnds 28–29 (28–30, 28–31): Ch 1; sc in each st around. Join with a sl st to first sc.

Rnd 30 (31, 32): Changing to smaller hook, ch 3 (counts as first dc); dc in each st around. Join with a sl st to third ch of beg ch-3. (72 [78, 84] dc)

Rnds 31–33 (32–34, 33–35): Ch 2 (does not count as dc); *fpdc around next 3 sts, bpdc around next 3 sts. Rep from * around. Join with a sl st to first fpdc. Finish off at end of Rnd 33 (34, 35).

Finishing

Weave in ends. Push all tr sts to RS of hat.

103

ski lift

SKILL LEVEL: EASY

O K, I admit it. This hat is not for everyone. But for any fun-loving, extroverted, and one-of-a-kind person, this is ideal. Go really crazy and add bells to the tassel! This is one of the longer, more time-consuming projects in this book, but so worth the time and effort involved.

Yarn

Spud and Chloe Fine (80% wool, 20% silk; 248 yds/227m per 2.3 oz/65g ball) or similar super fine weight yarn in colors:

> no. 7815 Red Hot (MC), 2 skeins

> no. 7817 Goldfish (CC1), 1 skein

> no. 7816 Dragonfly (CC2), 1 skein

Hooks and Notions

Size US G/6 (4mm) crochet hook or size needed to obtain gauge

Yarn needle

Finished Measurements

Men's S/M (Men's M/L):

22"–23" (55.9cm–58.4cm) (23"–24" [58.4cm–61cm])

Gauge

19 sts and 10 rows in dc = 4" (10.2cm)

✳ SPECIAL STITCHES

Magic Loop technique: See Stitch Glossary for details.

✳ PATTERN NOTES

First st in rnd is always worked in the same st as joining.

Ch 2 at beg of row is not counted as a st, unless stated. Ch these 2 sts loosely to the height of a dc.

CROCHET THE HAT

Rnd 1: With MC and starting with magic lp technique, ch 2; 12 dc in ring. Join with a sl st to first dc. (12 dc)

Rnds 2–4: Ch 2; dc in each st around. Join with a sl st to first dc.

Rnd 5: Ch 2; *dc in next 3 sts, 2 dc in next st. Rep from * around. Join with a sl st to first dc. (15 dc)

Rnds 6–9: Ch 2; dc in each st around. Join with a sl st to first dc.

Rnd 10: Ch 2; *dc in next 4 sts, 2 dc in next st. Rep from * around. Join with a sl st and CC1 to first dc. (18 dc)

Rnd 11: Ch 1; sc in first st, ch 2, sk 2 sts, *sc in next st, ch 2, sk 2 sts. Rep from * around. Join with sl st to first sc. Finish off. (6 sc and 6 ch-2 sps)

Rnd 12: Attach CC3 with a sl st to first ch-2 sp. Ch 2; working over ch-2 sp of previous rnd and into dc rnd before (Rnd 10) dc in next 3 dc. Ch 1, *dc into next 3 dc 2 rnds before, ch 1. Rep from * around. Finish off. (18 dc and 6 ch-1 sps)

Rnd 13: Attach CC2 with a sl st to first ch-1 sp. Ch 1; sc in same sp, ch 2. *Sc in next ch-1 sp, ch 2. Rep from * around. Join with a sl st to first sc. Finish off.

Rnds 14–15: Rep Rnds 12 and 13.

Rnd 16: Attach MC with a sl st to first ch-2 sp. Ch 2; working over ch-2 sp of previous rnd and into dc rnd before (Rnd 14) dc in next 2 dc, 2 dc in next dc. *Dc into next 2 dc 2 rnds before, 2 dc in next dc. Rep from * around. Join with a sl st to first dc. (24 dc)

Rnds 17–19: Ch 2; dc in each st around. Join with a sl st to first dc.

Rnd 20: Ch 2; *dc in next 3 sts, 2 dc in next st. Rep from * around. Join with a sl st to first dc. (30 dc)

Rnds 21–24: Ch 2; dc in each st around. Join with a sl st to first dc.

Rnd 25: Ch 2; *dc in next 4 sts, 2 dc in next st. Rep from * around. Join with a sl st and CC1 to first dc. (36 dc)

Rnds 26–30: Rep Rnds 11–15.

Rnd 31: Attach MC with a sl st to first ch-2 sp. Ch 2; working over ch-2 sp of previous rnd and into dc rnd before (Rnd 30) dc in next 2 dc, 2 dc in next dc. *Dc into next 2 dc 2 rnds before, 2 dc in next dc. Rep from * around. Join with a sl st to first dc. (48 dc)

Rnds 32–40: Ch 2; dc in each st around. Join with a sl st to first dc.

Rnds 41–45: Rep Rnds 11–15.

Rnds 46–90: Rep Rnds 31–45.

Rnd 91: Attach MC with a sl st to first ch-2 sp. Ch 2; working over ch-2 sp of previous rnd and into dc rnd before (round 90) dc in each dc around. This is not an increase row. (111 dc)

Rnds 92–95: Ch 2; dc in each st around. Join with a sl st to first dc.

Rnd 96: Ch 2; [dc in next 5 sts, dc dec over next 2 sts] 15 times. Dc in rem 6 sts. (96 dc)

Rnd 97: Ch 2; dc in each st around. Join with a sl st to first dc.

SIZE S
Rnd 98: Ch 2; [dc in next 6 sts, dc dec over next 2 sts] 12 times. (84 dc)

Rnd 99: Ch 2; dc in each st around. Join with a sl st to first dc.

Rnd 100: Ch 2; [dc in next 5 sts, dc dec over next 2 sts] 12 times. (72 dc)

SIZE M
Rnd 98: Ch 2; [dc in next 6 sts, dc dec over next 2 sts] 12 times. (84 dc)

Rnds 99–100: Ch 2; dc in each st around. Join with a sl st to first dc.

SIZE L
Rnds 98–100: Rep Rnd 97.

ALL SIZES
Rnd 101: Ch 2; *fpdc around next 2 sts, bpdc around next st. Rep from * around. Be sure to work around both parts of any dec st in previous row. Join with a sl st to first fpdc.

Rnds 102–106: Ch 2; *fpdc around next 2 fpdc, bpdc around next bpdc. Rep from * around. Join with a sl st to first fpdc. Join with CC1 at end of Rnd 106.

Rnd 107: Ch 2; *fpdc around next 2 fpdc, bpdc around next bpdc. Rep from * around. Join with a sl st and CC2 to first fpdc.

Rnds 108–110: Ch 2; *fpdc around next 2 fpdc, bpdc around next bpdc. Rep from * around. Join with a sl st to first fpdc. Finish off at end of Rnd 110.

Finishing

Weave in all ends. Make tassel body from CC2 approximately 6" (15.2cm) long. Wrap with CC1 multiple times. Use six 12" (30.5cm) strands of MC for attaching to hat. Braid these before attaching. Attach tassel to hat tip.

peak

Every man should have a classic beanie. The basic design and unlimited color choices allow you infinite creativity. The design includes a unique technique for creating the vertical stripe: unlike most hats, you will turn your work at the end of each round. Make sure you continue with the color changes to achieve the desired look.

Yarn

Tahki Cotton Classic Lite (100% mercerized cotton; 146 yds/135m per 1.8oz/50g ball) or similar light weight yarn in colors:

> no. 4017 Titanium (MC), 1 (1, 2) skein(s)
>
> no. 4405 Tangerine (CC1), 1 skein
>
> no. 4856 Deep Indigo (CC2), 1 skein

Hooks and Notions

Size US F/5 (3.75mm) crochet hook or size needed to obtain gauge

Yarn needle

Finished Measurements

Men's S (Men's M, Men's L):

22" (55.9cm) (23" [58.4cm], 24" [61cm])

Gauge

First 6 rows in pattern = 4" (10.2cm)

✳ SPECIAL STITCHES

Magic Loop technique: See Stitch Glossary for details.

✳ PATTERN NOTES

Ch 1 at beg of rnd does not count as a hdc.

Make ch 1 at beg of rnd loosely and pull to the height of a hdc.

Turn at the end of each rnd, unless stated otherwise in the pattern.

Always work CC1 in CC1 sts and never into MC sts. Do not continue color changes in last 2 rnds.

When working color changes you have two choices: 1) keep unused yarn ends on WS of work or 2) cut ends, being sure to leave enough to weave in.

CROCHET THE HAT

Rnd 1 (RS): Starting with MC and magic lp technique, ch 1; 6 hdc in lp, change to CC1, hdc in lp, change back to MC, hdc in lp. Join with a sl st to first hdc. Turn. (8 hdc)

Rnd 2: Ch 1; 2 hdc in each hdc around. Join with a sl st to first hdc. Turn. Be sure to continue with color changes. (16 hdc)

Rnd 3: Ch 1; *hdc in next st, 2 hdc in next st. Rep from * around. Join with a sl st to first hdc. Turn. (24 hc)

Rnd 4: Ch 1; *hdc in next 2 sts, 2 hdc in next st. Rep from * around. Join with a sl st to first hdc. Turn. (32 hdc)

Rnd 5: Ch 1; *hdc in next 3 sts, 2 hdc in next st. Rep from * around. Join with a sl st to first hdc. Turn. (40 hdc)

Rnd 6: Ch 1; *hdc in next 4 sts, 2 hdc in next st. Rep from * around. Join with a sl st to first hdc. Turn. (48 hdc)

Rnd 7: Ch 1; *hdc in next 5 sts, 2 hdc in next st. Rep from * around. Join with a sl st to first hdc. Turn. (56 hdc)

Rnd 8: Ch 1; *hdc in next 6 sts, 2 hdc in next st. Rep from * around. Join with a sl st to first hdc. Turn. (64 hdc)

Rnd 9: Ch 1; *hdc in next 7 sts, 2 hdc in next st. Rep from * around. Join with a sl st to first hdc. Turn. (72 hdc)

Rnd 10: Ch 1; *hdc in next 8 sts, 2 hdc in next st. Rep from * around. Join with a sl st to first hdc. Turn. (80 hdc)

Rnd 11: Ch 1; *hdc in next 9 sts, 2 hdc in next st. Rep from * around. Join with a sl st to first hdc. Turn. (88 total hdc, 11 in CC1)

SIZE M
Rnd 12: Ch 1; *hdc in next 21 sts, 2 hdc in next st. Rep from * around. Join with a sl st to first hdc. Turn. (92 total hdc, 11 in CC1)

SIZE L
Rnd 12: Ch 1; *hdc in next 22 sts, 2 hdc in next st. Rep from * around. Join with a sl st to first hdc. Turn. (96 total hdc, 12 in CC1)

ALL SIZES
Rnds 12–23 (13–25, 13–27): Ch 1; hdc in each st around. Join with a sl st to first hdc. Turn. (88 [92, 96] hdc)

Rnd 24 (26, 28): Ch 1; hdc in each st around. Join with a sl st and CC2 to first hdc. Turn. (88 [92, 96] hdc)

Rnds 25–26 (27–28, 29–30): Ch 1; sc in each st around. Join with a sl st to first sc. Do not turn. Finish off at end of Rnd 26 (28, 30).

Finishing

Weave in ends.

natural set

I love this set because the natural yarns used in the design are warm and organic, something that is very popular here in Colorado. The hat has a slightly slouchy design but fits snugly to the head, and the scarf perfectly completes the look. The thicker, bulky yarn allows this set to work up quickly.

Yarn

Cascade Yarns Ecological Wool (100% natural Peruvian wool; 478 yds/437m per 8.8 oz/250g ball) or similar bulky weight yarn in colors:

- no. 8087 Chocolate (MC), 1 skein

- no. 8015 Natural (CC), 1 skein

Hooks and Notions

Size US K/10.5 (6.5mm) crochet hook or size needed to obtain gauge

Yarn needle

Finished Measurements

Hat: Men's S (Men's M, Men's L):

22" (55.9cm) (23" [58.4cm], 24" [61cm])

Scarf: one size

78" × 6" (198.1cm × 15.2cm)

Gauge

For the hat: first 6 rnds in pattern = 4" (10.2cm)

For the scarf: 12 sts and 15 rows in sc = 4" (10.2cm)

✳ SPECIAL STITCHES

Magic Loop technique: See Stitch Glossary for details.

✳ PATTERN NOTES

For the hat, first st in rnd is always worked in the same st as joining.

Scarf is worked in 2 sections, working from the center out. Second side is attached to the unused lps of the beg ch.

CROCHET THE HAT

Rnd 1: With MC and starting with magic lp technique, ch 1; 6 sc in lp. Join with a sl st to first sc. (6 sc)

Rnd 2: Ch 1; 2 sc in each st around. Join with a sl st to first sc. (12 sc)

Rnd 3: Ch 1; *sc in next st, 2 sc in next st. Rep from * around. Join with a sl st to first sc. (18 sc)

Rnd 4: Ch 1; *sc in next 2 sts, 2 sc in next st. Rep from * around. Join with a sl st to first sc. (24 sc)

Rnd 5: Ch 1; *sc in next 3 sts, 2 sc in next st. Rep from * around. Join with a sl st to first sc. (30 sc)

Rnd 6: Ch 1; *sc in next 4 sts, 2 sc in next st. Rep from * around. Join with a sl st to first sc. (36 sc)

Rnd 7: Ch 1; *sc in next 5 sts, 2 sc in next st. Rep from * around. Join with a sl st to first sc. (42 sc)

Rnd 8: Ch 1; *sc in next 6 sts, 2 sc in next st. Rep from * around. Join with a sl st to first sc. (48 sc)

Rnd 9: Ch 1; *sc in next 7 sts, 2 sc in next st. Rep from * around. Join with a sl st to first sc. (54 sc)

Rnd 10: Ch 1; *sc in next 8 sts, 2 sc in next st. Rep from * around. Join with a sl st to first sc. (60 sc)

Rnd 11: Ch 1; *sc in next 9 sts, 2 sc in next st. Rep from * around. Join with a sl st to first sc. (66 sc)

SIZE M AND L

Rnd 12: Ch 1; *sc in next 10 sts, 2 sc in next st. Rep from * around. Join with a sl st to first sc. (72 sc)

SIZE L

Rnd 13: Ch 1; *sc in next 11 sts, 2 sc in next st. Rep from * around. Join with a sl st to first sc. (78 sc)

Begin Colorwork Section

Rnd 12 (13, 14): Ch 1; *sc in next st, sk 2 sts, 5 dc in next st, sk 2 sts. Rep from * around. Join with a sl st and CC to first sc.

Rnd 13 (14, 15): Ch 2; dc2tog over next 2 sts, ch 2, sc in next st. *Ch 2, dc5tog over next 5 sts, ch 2, sc in next st. Rep from * around until 2 sts rem. Ch 2, dc2tog over last 2 sts. Join with a sl st and MC to first dc2tog.

Rnd 14 (15, 16): Ch 1; *sc in dc5tog of previous rnd, 5 dc in next sc. Rep from * around. Join with a sl st and CC to first sc.

Rnds 15–18 (16–19, 17–20): Rep Rnds 13–14 (14–15, 15–16).

Rnd 19 (20, 21): Rep Rnd 14 (15, 16).

Rnd 20 (21, 22): Ch 1; sc in each sc and 2 sc in each ch-2 sp around. Join with a sl st to first sc. (66 [72, 78] sc)

Rnd 21 (22, 23): Ch 2 (does not count as a st); dc in each st around. Join with a sl st to first dc.

Rnd 22 (23, 24): Ch 2; fpdc around each dc around. Join with a sl st to first fpdc.

Rnds 23–26 (24–27, 25–28): Ch 2, fpdc around each fpdc around. Join with a sl st to first fpdc. Finish off at end of Row 26 (27, 28).

Finishing

Weave in all ends.

CROCHET THE SCARF

Row 1 (RS): With MC, loosely ch 20.
Sc in second ch from hook and each ch across.
Turn. (19 sc)

Rows 2–88: Ch 1; sc in each st across. Turn.

Row 89: Ch 3; 2 dc in first st, sk 2 sts,
sc in next st, [sk 2 sts, 5 dc in next st, sk 2 sts,
sc in next st] 2 times. Sk 2 sts, 3 dc in last
st changing to CC. Turn.

Row 90: Ch 1; sc in first st, [ch 2, dc5tog over
next 5 sts, ch 2, sc in next st] 3 times. Change
to MC. Turn.

Row 91: Ch 3; 2 dc in same st, [5 dc in next
sc, sc in next dc5tog] 2 times. 3 dc in last
st changing to CC. Turn.

Rows 92–97: Rep Rows 90 and 91.

Row 98: Ch 1; sc in each st and
ch-2 sp across. Turn. (19 sc)

Rows 99–100: Ch 1; sc in each st across.
Turn. Finish off at end of Row 100.

Second side

Row 1: With RS and Row 1 of previous side
facing, attach MC with a sl st to first unused
lp on the opposite side of the original ch. Ch 1;
sc in each st across. Turn. (19 sc)

Rows 2–100: Rep the same as first side.

Finishing

Weave in all ends.

stitch glossary

bet – between

beg – beginning

BL – back loop

bpdc – back post double crochet

CC – contrast color

ch(s) – chain(s)

CL – cluster

cm - centimeter

dec – decrease

dc – double crochet

FL – front loop

fpdc – front post double crochet

fphdc – front post half double crochet

fptr – front post treble crochet

fsc – foundation single crochet

g – grams

hdc – half double crochet

hhdc – herringbone half double crochet

in – inches

lp(s) – loop(s)

m – meter

mm – millimeter

MC – main color

oz – ounce

rem – remaining

rep – repeat

rnd(s) – round(s)

RS – right side

rev sc – reverse single crochet

sc – single crochet

sl st – slip stitch

sk – skip

sp(s) – space(s)

st(s) – stitch(es)

tr – treble crochet

tog – together

WS – wrong side

yd(s) – yard(s)

YO – yarn over

BASIC STITCHES

Once you've mastered these basic stitches, you'll be ready to make most of the hats in this book.

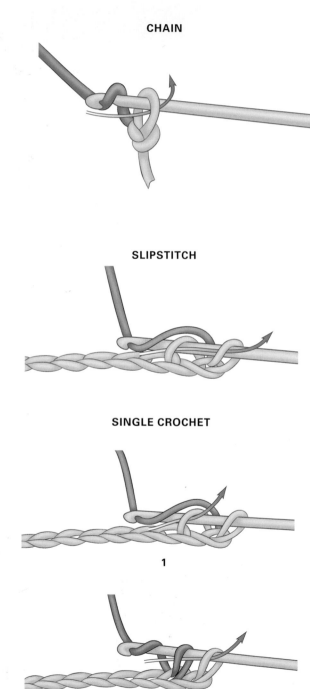

CHAIN

SLIPSTITCH

SINGLE CROCHET

1

2

DOUBLE CROCHET

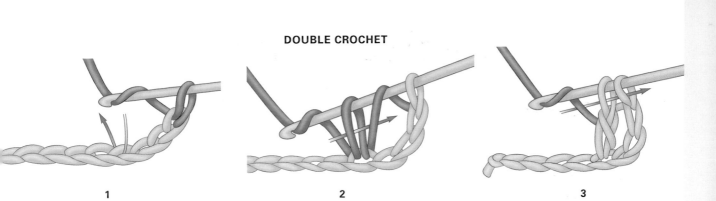

1   2   3

HALF DOUBLE CROCHET

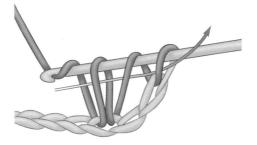

TREBLE CROCHET

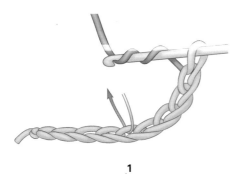

1   2

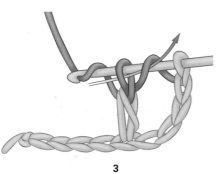

3   4

These stitches are slightly more advanced, but are well worth the extra effort.

MAGIC LOOP

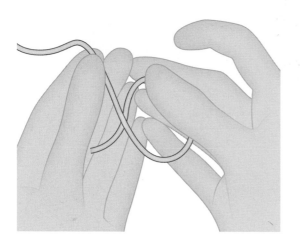

1 Leaving a tail 6" (15.2cm) or longer, create a lp by placing the tail behind the yarn coming from your skein or ball.

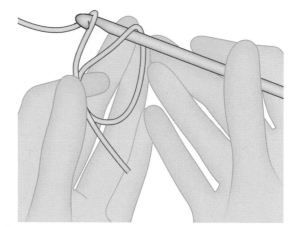

2 Keeping a firm hold on the long tail and lp, insert your hook through the lp and YO.

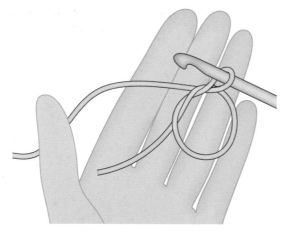

3 Pull a lp up through the lp.

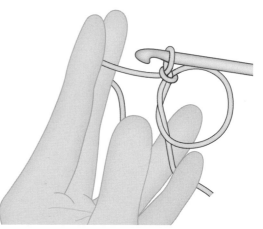

4 Ch the necessary number and work sts into the ring by inserting the hook through the ring and completing the st as usual. Continue working sts over the tail and into the magic lp. Once all sts are completed, firmly grasp the tail and pull tightly until the hole is gone. Continue as pattern states.

BACK LOOP AND FRONT LOOP

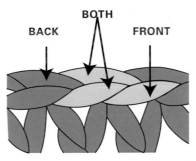

Most crochet sts are worked under both lps of a st. Sometimes a pattern will tell you to work into the BL or FL only.

WORKING IN BACK HUMP

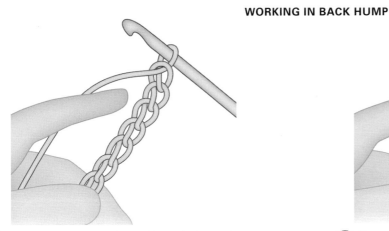

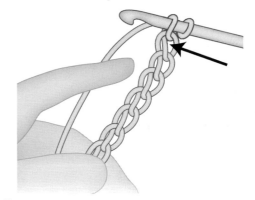

1 Create the desired number of chs and turn the ch over so the "back" is now facing you. The middle thread creates a "hump" on the back of the chain.

2 Insert the hook under the hump created by the middle thread and finish the stitch as usual.

CHANGING COLORS

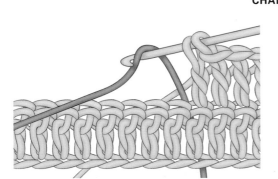

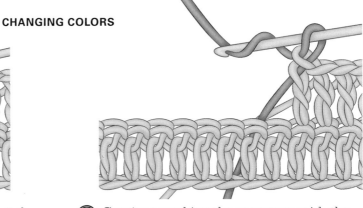

1 Before completing the last YO of the st, switch colors, pulling the new color through the sts still on the hook.

2 Continue working the st pattern with the new color.

FOUNDATION SINGLE CROCHET

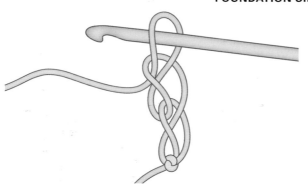

1 Starting with a slipknot on hook, ch 2.

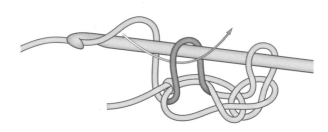

2 Insert hook in the second ch from hook, and pull up a lp.

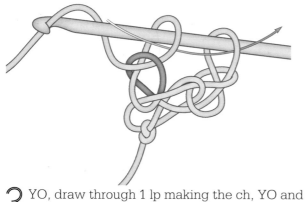

3 YO, draw through 1 lp making the ch, YO and draw through 2 lps making the sc.

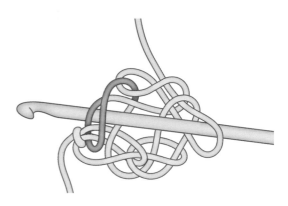

4 *Insert your hook under 2 loops of the chain stitch of the last stitch.

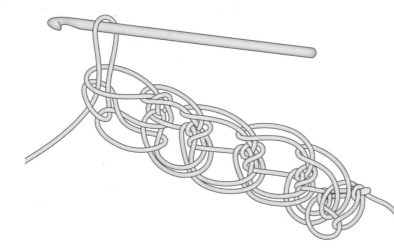

5 Pull up a loop, YO and draw through 1 loop, YO and draw through 2 loops. Repeat from * for number of stitches desired. Fsc made.

BACK POST DOUBLE CROCHET

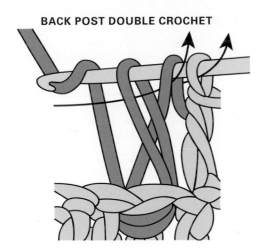

YO, insert hook from back to front to back around post of stitch below, YO and pull up lp [YO, draw through 2 loops on hook] 2 times. Bpdc made.

CLUSTER

[YO, insert hook into st and draw up a lp to the height of a dc, YO and draw through 2 lps on hook] 2 times, YO and draw through all 3 lps on hook. Cl made.

FRONT POST DOUBLE CROCHET

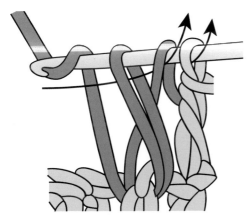

YO, insert hook from front to back to front around post of st below, YO and pull up a loop, [YO and draw through 2 lps on hook] 2 times. Fpdc made.

FRONT POST TREBLE CROCHET

YO 2 times, insert hook from front to back to front around the post of st below, YO and pull up lp, [YO, draw through 2 lps on hook] 3 times. Fptc made.

HERRINGBONE HALF DOUBLE CROCHET

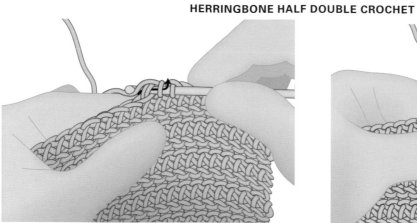
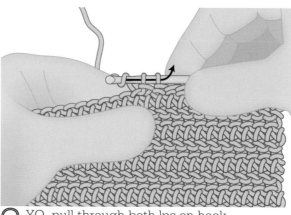

1 YO, insert hook into st, pull through st and first lp on hook.

2 YO, pull through both lps on hook. Hhdc made.

REVERSE SINGLE CROCHET

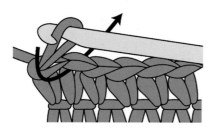
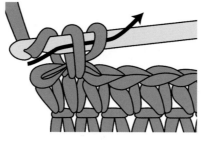
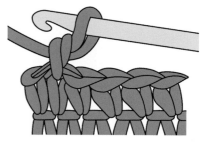

1 Working from left to right, insert hook into stitch and pull up lp.

2 YO and draw this lp through the first lp to join.

3 *Insert hook in next stitch to right, pull up a lp, YO, and draw through both lps on hook; repeat from * for desired number of stitches. Rev sc made.

metric conversion chart

TO CONVERT	TO	MULTIPLY BY
Inches	Centimeters	2.54
Centimeters	Inches	0.4
Feet	Centimeters	30.5
Centimeters	Feet	0.03
Yards	Meters	0.9
Meters	Yards	1.1

index

www.fwmedia.com

18   17   16   15   14   5   4   3   2   1

DISTRIBUTED IN CANADA BY FRASER DIRECT

100 Armstrong Avenue

Georgetown, ON, Canada L7G 5S4

Tel: (905) 877-4411

DISTRIBUTED IN THE U.K. AND EUROPE BY F&W MEDIA INTERNATIONAL

Brunel House, Newton Abbot, Devon, TQ12 4PU, England

Tel: (+44) 1626 323200, Fax: (+44) 1626 323319

Email: enquiries@fwmedia.com

DISTRIBUTED IN AUSTRALIA BY CAPRICORN LINK

P.O. Box 704, S. Windsor NSW, 2756 Australia

Tel: (02) 4560 1600, Fax: (02) 4577 5288

E-mail: books@capricornlink.com.au

ISBN-13: 978-1-4402-3976-2

ISBN-10: 1-4402-3976-2

SRN: T0020

Edited by Stephanie White

Designed by Michelle Thompson

Production coordinated by Greg Nock

Photography by Cat Mayer

about the author

Jennifer J. Cirka is the designer behind Jaybird Designs and a Crochet Guild of America recognized Professional Crochet Designer. She is also a regular contributor to magazines such as *Crochet World* and *Crochet! Magazine*. Her independently published crochet patterns are sold online; visit www.jaybirddesigns.com for more information. Jennifer, a homeschooling mom, lives with her family and two retired Greyhounds in Grand Junction, Colorado. When not crocheting and designing, she enjoys camping, hiking, baking, and selling real estate.

In Loving Memory of:

My grandma, Martha Jean Hardway. Thanks for passing down your creative genes and for instilling in me a love of all things crafty, including my first crochet lessons. I'll always remember our fun New Years' Eves full of Dick Clark, dancing, homemade peanut butter fudge and Monopoly. Miss you!

My dad, Gary L. Chalupiak. Thanks for always believing in me and teaching me that I can accomplish anything I set my mind to. Thanks for bringing me to Colorado, too. Wish you were here!

acknowledgments

I have many people at F+W Media who helped me through this adventure of writing my first crochet book. Thank you to Amelia Johanson who fought so hard for my ideas to become a reality. Also, to Stephanie White, my editor, thank you for being a wonderful support. A huge thanks to everyone else at F+W who had a hand in making my book attractive and comprehensible.

I need to thank all the local people who helped give my book the outdoorsy, Colorado lifestyle look and feel. It was such a pleasure to get to know Cat Mayer of Cat Mayer Photography. Your astonishingly gorgeous photographs brought my designs to life. Also, thank you for introducing me to my amazing models; the Davis Family, the Hansow Family, the Balsamo Family, and the Brown Family. A special thanks also goes to Miss Kathryn Dunaway for her impromptu modeling of the Rainbow Hat. I treasure all your patience while modeling and it was so nice to meet all of you. Thanks for being such adorable, photogenic, families!

I want to send hugs and blessings to all of my friends and family who cheered me on through this adventure; the Mom's In Training group, the Providence 4H group, and my friends at Celebrate Recovery and Step Study at Canyon View Vineyard Church. Huge thank you's to my mom, Nannette Chalupiak, my sister, Linda McCoy, and my "other sister" Cora Sykes for being supportive, encouraging, and proud of me each and every time we talked.

And last, but certainly not least, I could not have accomplished this dream of mine without the love and support of my awesome husband, Ron and my beautiful daughter, Heather. Ron, I appreciate your encouragement and forgiveness; Heather, thanks for putting up with all my requests to try on hats; and for both of your creative ideas and suggestions. This book would not have be possible without you. I love you both!

Keep on Crocheting!

Blooming Crochet Hats
10 Crochet Designs With 10 Mix-and-Match Accents

SHAUNA-LEE GRAHAM

Blooming Crochet Hats features a variety of hat patterns for crocheters of all skill levels. The ten interchangeable motifs (including bears, hearts, butterflies, rabbits and an assortment of colorful crochet flowers) make these projects fun, fashionable and unique to each wearer.

Go Crochet! Skillbuilder
30 Crochet-in-a-Day Projects to Take You From Beginner to Expert

ELLEN GORMLEY

Go Crochet! Skillbuilder is perfect for crocheters interested in learning new techniques quickly. Each skill-building project can be completed quickly and will progress your crochet knowledge at the same time. Work through all 30 projects and you'll be an expert in no time!